T0233351

Agile Android

Godfrey Nolan

Apress®

Agile Android

ISBN-13 (pbk): 978-1-4842-9700-1

ISBN-13 (electronic): 978-1-4842-9701-8

Managing Director: Welmoed Spahr
Lead Editor: Steve Anglin
Technical Reviewers: Travis Himes and Tri Phan
Editorial Board: Steve Anglin, Ewan Buckingham, Gary Cornell, Louise Corrigan, James T. DeWolf,
    Jonathan Gennick, Jonathan Hassell, Robert Hutchinson, Michelle Lowman, James Markham,
    Matthew Moodie, Jeff Olson, Jeffrey Pepper, Douglas Pundick, Ben Renow-Clarke,
    Dominic Shakeshaft, Gwenan Spearing, Matt Wade, Steve Weiss
Coordinating Editor: Mark Powers
Copy Editor: Lori Jacobs
Compositor: SPi Global
Indexer: SPi Global
Artist: SPi Global

Distributed to the book trade worldwide by Springer Science+Business Media New York, 233 Spring Street, 6th Floor, New York, NY 10013. Phone 1-800-SPRINGER, fax (201) 348-4505, e-mail orders-ny@springer-sbm.com, or visit www.springeronline.com. Apress Media, LLC is a California LLC and the sole member (owner) is Springer Science + Business Media Finance Inc (SSBM Finance Inc). SSBM Finance Inc is a Delaware corporation.

For information on translations, please e-mail rights@apress.com, or visit www.apress.com.

Apress and friends of ED books may be purchased in bulk for academic, corporate, or promotional use. eBook versions and licenses are also available for most titles. For more information, reference our Special Bulk Sales–eBook Licensing web page at www.apress.com/bulk-sales.

Any source code or other supplementary material referenced by the author in this text is available to readers at www.apress.com/9781484297001. For detailed information about how to locate your book's source code, go to www.apress.com/source-code/. Readers can also access source code at SpringerLink in the Supplementary Material section for each chapter.

For Dad.
Great teacher, great golfer, great dad.
You will be sorely missed.

Contents at a Glance

Contents

About the Author

Godfrey Nolan is founder and president of RIIS LLC, a mobile development firm in the Detroit Metro area. He is also author of *Bulletproof Android* (Addison-Wesley Professional, 2014), *Android Best Practices* (Apress, 2014), *Decompiling Java* (Apress, 2004) and *Decompiling Android* (Apress, 2012). Originally from Dublin, Ireland he now lives in Huntington Woods, MI.

About the Technical Reviewers

Travis Himes is a Senior Software Engineer specializing in Android development with more than 12 years of experience. Travis has given talks at the Philadelphia Android Alliance, and has taught fellow developers and developers-in-training the basics of Android development. Travis is a fan of keyboard shortcuts, and really anything that saves time and increases repeatability. If there is an opportunity for learning something new, he's likely to be involved.

Tri Phan is the founder of the Programming Learning Channel on YouTube. He has over seven years of experience in the software industry. Specifically, he has worked for many outsourcing companies and has written applications in a variety of programming languages such as PHP, Java, and C#. In addition, he has over six years of experience in teaching at international and technological centers such as Aptech, NIIT, and Kent College.

Acknowledgments

There are many people I'd like to thank for helping me write this book.
Apologies if I've forgotten anyone.

- Travis Himes, for quickly stepping in to review the book at the last minute.

- David Armstrong, Tom Kocik and Nathan Baumgartner who helped me with the code samples.

- Mark Powers and Steve Anglin at Apress. And yes I know I'm late again.

- My beautiful wife, Nancy, for putting up with me when I needed to talk about what I was writing.

- The many bored listeners at way too many conferences who provided great feedback that helped shape the content of this book over the past couple years.

Chapter 1

Introduction

For a while now, Agile development has been problematic for Android developers. There have been a number of ways to test the user interface (UI), such as Robotium or Monkey Runner, but before Android Studio 1.1, unit testing was hard to use, hard to configure, and quite challenging to implement on the Android platform.

Google would argue, no doubt, that in the past you could use JUnit3-style unit testing. But for anyone from classic Java development this was a dramatic backward step in time. Developers would stumble along hacking together a JUnit4 development environment using a number of third-party tools. More likely than not they would simply give up as the ever-increasing series of mutually incompatible library dependencies would finally wear them down. Because there simply wasn't the toolbox for the Android developer, Agile development on the mobile platform was immature and reminiscent of Java development in the early 2000s.

Thankfully all this has changed - Android now supports JUnit4 and Android developers can now return to unit testing. It's early days yet in the world of Android JUnit4 testing world and the documentation is thin on the ground, so in this book we're going to show practical ways to get your unit testing up and running using Android Studio. We'll also look at how this can be complemented by other UI-specific Android testing libraries such as Espresso to create a complete Agile testing framework for Android developers.

Hello, World Unit Test

Before we go any further let's look at a simple unit test. For demonstration purposes we can use the Add method from the Google Calculator example, which is available from `https://github.com/googlesamples/android-testing` (see Listing 1-1).

Listing 1-1. Add Method from Google's Calculator Example

```
public double add(double firstOperand, double secondOperand) {
    return firstOperand + secondOperand;
}
```

Listing 1-2 shows a very simple unit test, which tests if the Add method can add two numbers correctly.

Listing 1-2. Test Method for Add Method from Calculator Example

```
@Test
public void calculator_CorrectAdd_ReturnsTrue() {
    double resultAdd = mCalculator.add(3, 4);
    assertEquals(7, resultAdd, 0);
}
```

Unit tests use assertions to make sure the method provides an expected result. In this case we're using `assertEquals` to see if the Add method returns 7 when adding 3 to 4. If the test works, then we should see a positive or green result, and if it doesn't, then we'll see a red result in Android Studio.

Understand the Benefits of Using an Agile Approach to Android Development

If you're new to Agile development you're probably wondering how Agile can improve the development process.

At its most basic, Agile, and unit testing in particular, helps you to

- Catch more mistakes, earlier in the development process

- Confidently make more changes

- Build in regression testing

- Extend the life of your codebase

If you write unit tests and they cover a significant portion of your code then you're going to catch more bugs. You can make simple changes to tidy up the code or more extensive architectural changes, run your unit tests, and, if they all pass, be confident that you didn't introduce any subtle defects. The more unit tests you write, the more you can regression test your app whenever you change the code without fear. And once you have a lot of unit tests, then it becomes a regression test suite that allows you to have the confidence to do things you wouldn't otherwise attempt.

Unit tests mean you no longer have to program with a "leave well enough alone" mind-set. You can now make significant changes (changing to a new database, updating your back-end application programming interface (API), changing to a new material design theme, etc.) and be confident that your app is behaving the same as before you made the changes since all the tests execute without any errors.

Explore the Agile Testing Pyramid for Android

There are several types of tests you need in your test suite to make sure your app is fully tested. You should have Unit Tests for the component- or method-level functionality, API or Acceptance Tests for any back-end RESTful APIs, and GUI (graphical user interface) Tests for Android activities and general application workflow.

The classic Agile Test Pyramid first appeared in Succeeding with Agile *by Mike Cohn (*Pearson Education, 2010). This is a good guide for the relative quantity of each type of test your app is going to need (see Figure 1-1).

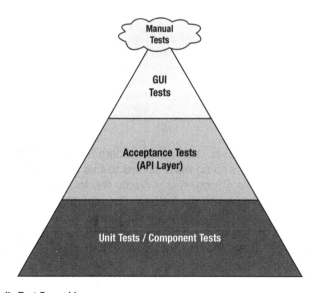

Figure 1-1. Agile Test Pyramid

Create Hello World Unit Test in Android

In the following example we show how to create our simple unit test example in Android Studio. This should return true assuming adding two numbers in the calculator Android app works correctly.

To set up and run a unit test you need to perform the following tasks:

- Prerequisites: Android Plugin for Gradle version 1.1.x

- Create the `src/test/java` folders

- Add JUnit:4:12 dependency in `build.gradle` (app) file

- Choose unit tests' test artifact in Build Variant

- Create unit tests

- Right-click tests to run tests

Click File ➤ Project Structure and make sure the Android Plugin version is greater than 1.1. In Figure 1-2 the Android Plugin version is 1.2.3 so we're good to go.

		Project Structure
+ −	Gradle version	2.2.1
SDK Location	Android Plugin Version	1.2.3
Project	Android Plugin Repository	jcenter
Developer Services	Default Library Repository	jcenter
Ads		
Analytics		
Authentication		
Notifications		
Modules		
app		

Figure 1-2.

Next we need to create the `src/test/java` folders for our unit test code. For the moment this seems to be hard-coded to this directory. So change to Project view to see the file structure and create the folders (see Figure 1-3). Alternatively, in Windows create the folders using the file explorer or on a Mac use the command line on a terminal window to make the changes. Don't be worried if the folders don't show up when you go back to the Android view in Android Studio. They'll show up when we change to unit tests in the Build Variant window.

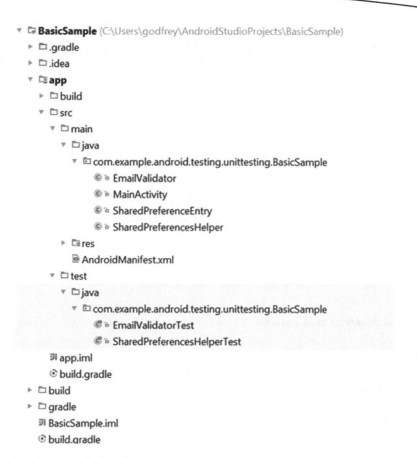

Figure 1-3. Change to Project view

Add junit library to the dependencies section in the build.gradle (app) file as shown in Figure 1-4.

```
apply plugin: 'com.android.application'

android {
    compileSdkVersion 22
    buildToolsVersion '22.0.1'
    defaultConfig {
        applicationId "com.example.android.testing.unittesting.BasicSample"
        minSdkVersion 8
        versionCode 1
        versionName "1.0"
        targetSdkVersion 22
    }
    productFlavors {
    }
}

dependencies {
    // Unit testing dependencies.
    testCompile 'junit:junit:4.12'
    testCompile 'org.mockito:mockito-core:1.10.19'
}
```

Figure 1-4. Modify the build.gradle file

Choose the Unit Tests test artifact in Build Variants and use the debug build (see Figure 1-5). The test code directory should now also appear when you're in the Android view of your app.

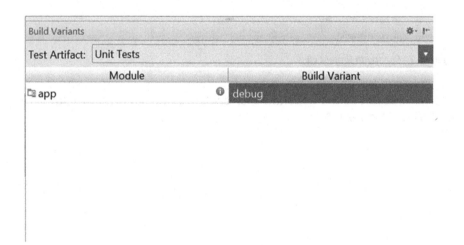

Figure 1-5. Choose Unit Tests in Build Variant

Create the Unit Tests code for our simple example. We need to import the org.junit.Before so we can create a Calculator object. We need to import org.junit.Test to tell Android Studio that we're doing unit tests. And as we're going to do an assertEquals, we also need to import org.junit. Assert.assertEquals (see Listing 1-3).

Listing 1-3. Unit Test Code

```
package com.riis.calculatoradd;

import org.junit.Before;
import org.junit.Test;

import static org.junit.Assert.assertEquals;

public class CalculatorTest {

    private Calculator mCalculator;

    @Before
    public void setUp() {
        mCalculator = new Calculator();
    }

    @Test
    public void calculator_CorrectAdd_ReturnsTrue() {
        double resultAdd = mCalculator.add(3, 4);
        assertEquals("adding 3 + 4 didn't work this time", 7, resultAdd , 0);
        }
    }
```

Right-click the CalculatorTest java file and choose Run 'CalculatorTest' to run tests (see Figure 1-6).

Figure 1-6. *Running the unit test*

You can see the results of the tests in the Run windows (see Figure 1-7). You may also want to click the configuration gear and choose Show Statistics to see how long the tests take.

Figure 1-7. *Test results*

If your tests are successful they show as green, and anything that produces an error is shown in red. All your tests should be green before you continue with any coding.

GUI Tests

The real beauty of unit testing is that you don't need an emulator or physical device to do your testing. But, if we look back at our Agile Testing Pyramid (Figure 1-1) we know that we're going to need some GUI tests. Remember, GUI tests are tests on Activities and unit tests are tests on individual methods in your code. We won't need as many GUI tests as unit tests, but we're still going to have to test every activity for happy paths as well as not so happy paths.

When it comes to testing GUI we have a few frameworks that we can choose from: we can use the Android JUnit3 framework, Google's Espresso, UIAutomator, Robotium, or some Cucumber-type Android framework such as Calabash. In this book we'll use Google's Espresso as it's quick and easy to set up and it also has support for Gradle and Android Studio. But your author has used the other frameworks in the past and they all have their benefits.

Espresso has three components: ViewMatchers, ViewActions, and ViewAssertions. ViewMatchers are used to find a view, ViewActions allow you to do something with a view, and ViewAssertions are similar to unit test assertions—they let you assert that the value in the view is what you'd expect or not.

Listing 1-4 shows a simple example of an Espresso GUI test. We're adding two numbers again, but this time we're doing it by interacting with the GUI, not calling the underlying method.

Listing 1-4. Adding Two Numbers Using Espresso

```
public void testCalculatorAdd() {

    onView(withId(R.id.operand_one_edit_text)).perform(typeText(THREE));
    onView(withId(R.id.operand_two_edit_text)).perform(typeText(FOUR));
    onView(withId(R.id.operation_add_btn)).perform(click());
    onView(withId(R.id.operation_result_text_view)).check(matches(withText
    (RESULT)));
}
```

In this example withId(R.id.operand_one_edit_text) is one of the ViewMatchers in the code and perform(typeText(THREE) is a ViewAction. Finally check(matches(withText(RESULT)) is the ViewAssertion.

Create Hello, World GUI Test

This time we show how to create our simple GUI test example in Android Studio. As with the unit test, this one should return true assuming that adding two numbers in the calculator Android app works correctly.

To set up and run a GUI test you need to perform the following tasks:

- Prerequisites: install the Android Support Repository
- Put the test classes in the src/androidTest/java folders
- Add Espresso dependency in build.gradle (app) file

- Choose Android Test Instrumentation Test Artifact in Build Variant

- Create GUI tests

- Right-click tests to run tests

Click Tools ➤ Android ➤ SDK Manager, click the SDK tools tab, and make sure the Android Support Repository is installed (see Figure 1-8).

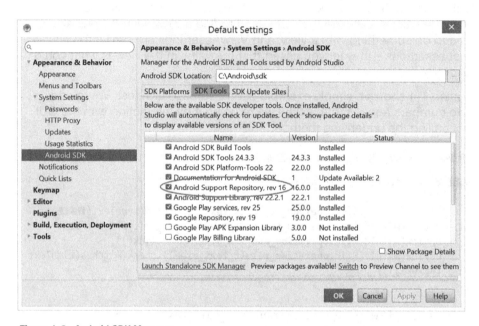

Figure 1-8. Android SDK Manager

By default, Android Studio creates a `src/androidTest/java` folder when you create the project using the project wizard so you shouldn't have to create any new directory. If you can't see it, then check that the Test Artifact in the Build Variant window is set to Android Instrumentation Tests (see Figure 1-9).

Figure 1-9. Build Variant test artifacts

Add the following Espresso libraries (see Listing 1-5) to the build.gradle (app) file in the dependencies section and click the Sync Now link. Open the Gradle console as this may take a minute or two.

Listing 1-5. Espresso Libraries

```
dependencies {
    androidTestCompile 'com.android.support.test:testing-support-lib:0.1'
    androidTestCompile 'com.android.support.test.espresso:espresso-core:2.0'
}
```

The code in Listing 1-6 shows how we set up and run the GUI test to add 3 + 4 and how we assert that this is 7.0. In order to test Android activities we need to extend the CalculatorAddTest with the ActivityInstrumentationTestCase2 class. This allows you to take control of the activities. We do this in the setUp() method using the getActivity() call.

Listing 1-6. Adding Two numbers Using Espresso

```
import android.test.ActivityInstrumentationTestCase2;

import static android.support.test.espresso.Espresso.onView;
import static android.support.test.espresso.action.ViewActions.click;
import static android.support.test.espresso.action.ViewActions.typeText;
import static android.support.test.espresso.assertion.ViewAssertions.matches;
import static android.support.test.espresso.matcher.ViewMatchers.withId;
import static android.support.test.espresso.matcher.ViewMatchers.withText;

public class CalculatorAddTest extends ActivityInstrumentationTestCase2<
CalculatorActivity> {
```

```
public static final String THREE = "3";
public static final String FOUR = "4";
public static final String RESULT = "7.0";

public CalculatorAddTest() {
    super(CalculatorActivity.class);
}

@Override
protected void setUp() throws Exception {
    super.setUp();
    getActivity();
}

public void testCalculatorAdd() {

    onView(withId(R.id.operand_one_edit_text)).perform(typeText(THREE));
    onView(withId(R.id.operand_two_edit_text)).perform(typeText(FOUR));
    onView(withId(R.id.operation_add_btn)).perform(click());
    onView(withId(R.id.operation_result_text_view)).check(matches
    (withText(RESULT)));
}
}
```

In the code we first connect to the Calculator Activity and then use the ViewMatcher and ViewActions to put the numbers 3 and 4 in the correct text fields. The code then uses a ViewAction to click the Add button and finally we use the ViewAssertion to make sure the answer is the expected 7.0. Note that the GUI displays the result as a double, so it's 7.0 and not 7 as you might expect (see Figure 1-10).

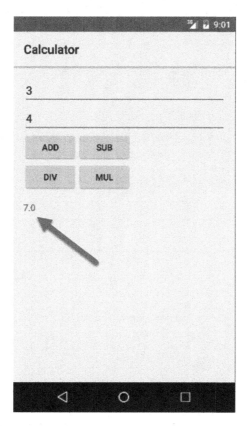

Figure 1-10. *Calculator app*

Figure 1-11 shows the results. In this case they look very similar to those in the unit tests, but it took a lot longer for the emulator to spin up.

Figure 1-11. *Espresso results*

Summary

In this chapter we looked at the current state of unit testing and GUI tests on the Android platform. In the rest of this book we'll explore Agile testing in a lot more detail so you can see how to apply these techniques to your application to produce cleaner, faster code with fewer defects.

Chapter 2

Android Unit Testing

Before Android Studio incorporated JUnit4, Google's implementation was an odd mix of standard and Android-specific unit tests. The current version of JUnit4 is a much more vanilla implementation of the JUnit standard (see `http://junit.org` for more information or `https://github.com/junit-team/junit` for the source code). The current recommended version of JUnit we're loading in the build.gradle file is 4.12

Android Assertions

In our Hello, World example we used the `assertEquals` assertion, but there are other assertions in JUnit 4.12 that we can use (see Table 2-1).

Table 2-1. Assertions

Assertion	Description
assertEquals	Test that two values are the same
assertTrue	Test Boolean condition is true
assertFalse	Test Boolean condition is false
assertNull	Check that the object is null
assertNotNull	Check that the object is not null
assertSame	Test that both values refer to the same object reference
assertNotSame	Test that both values do not refer to the same object reference
assertThat	Test that the first value (object) matches the second value (or matcher)
fail	Test should always fail

There are also many other asserts that you can use if you add Hamcrest, AssertJ, or any of the many other assert libraries. But for the moment let's start with the basic JUnit assertions.

`assertTrue` and `assertFalse` are used when you're looking to check the value of a Boolean condition. Rather than having to `assertTrue(!something YouExpectToReturnFalse)`, `assertFalse` is provided (e.g., `assertTrue (5 < 6)` and `assertFalse (5>6)`).

`assertNull` and `assertNotNull` check to see if an object is null (e.g., `assertNull(Calculator)` or `assertNotNull(Calculator)`).

`assertSame` and `assertNotSame` check that the two objects are references to the same object for `assertSame` or not for `assertNotSame`. This is not the same as equals, which compares the values of the two objects and not the object itself.

`assertThat` can be used like `assertEquals` where instead of saying `assertEquals(7, mCalculator.add(3,4), 0)` we can now say `assertThat(is(7), mCalculator.add(3, 4))`.

`fail` is for simply a failing test, for code that never should have been reached or to tell you "here be dragons."

Command Line

Unit tests can be run from the command line using the following command: `gradlew test --continue`. The `gradlew` task runs the unit tests and continue tells `gradlew` not to stop if any of the unit tests fail, which is what we want.

```
C:\AndroidStudioProjects\BasicSample>gradlew test --continue
Downloading https://services.gradle.org/distributions/gradle-2.2.1-all.zip
.......................................................................
.............................................
Unzipping C:\Users\godfrey\.gradle\wrapper\dists\gradle-2.2.1-
all\6dibv5rcnnqlfbq9klf8imrndn\gradle-2.2.1-all.zip to C:\Users\godfrey\.
gradle\wrapper\dists\gradle-2.2.1-all\6dibv5rcnnqlfbq9klf8imrndn
Download https://jcenter.bintray.com/com/google/guava/guava/17.0/guava-
17.0.jar
Download https://jcenter.bintray.com/com/android/tools/lint/lint-api/24.2.3/
lint-api-24.2.3.jar
Download https://jcenter.bintray.com/org/ow2/asm/asm-analysis/5.0.3/asm-
analysis-5.0.3.jar
Download https://jcenter.bintray.com/com/android/tools/external/lombok/
lombok-ast/0.2.3/lombok-ast-0.2.3.jar
:app:preBuild UP-TO-DATE
:app:preDebugBuild UP-TO-DATE
```

```
:app:checkDebugManifest
:app:prepareDebugDependencies
:app:compileDebugAidl
:app:compileDebugRenderscript
.
.
.
:app:compileReleaseUnitTestSources
:app:assembleReleaseUnitTest
:app:testRelease
:app:test

BUILD SUCCESSFUL

Total time: 3 mins 57.013 secs
```

You may want to run your tests from the command line, especially the first time you run a unit test, using the `gradlew test --continue` command so that you can see what's happening, or alternatively open the gradle console in Android Studio. Otherwise you may end up wondering why nothing is happening as Android Studio downloads all the necessary files to run unit tests.

Command-line test execution is also very useful if you're using a continuous integration build tool such as Jenkins.

JUnit Options

JUnit4 has the following annotations

- @Before

- @After

- @Test

- @BeforeClass

- @AfterClass

- @Test(timeout=ms)

@Test is used to annotate all test methods (see Listing 2-1), without it, the method will not be run as a test. @Test(timeout=ms) is a slight wrinkle on the standard annotation; it simply says give up if the test is taking longer than the defined timeout given in milliseconds.

Listing 2-1. @Test Method

```java
@Test
public void calculator_CorrectSub_ReturnsTrue() {
    assertEquals(1, mCalculator.sub(4, 3),0);
}
```

@Before and @After are used for any setup and teardown functions that you're going to need. For example, @Before could include code to write to log files or create objects to be used in the test or perhaps open the database and then seed the database with test data. @After is typically used to reverse any of those @Before changes, such as deleting the test rows in the database, and so on (see Listing 2-2).

Listing 2-2. @Before and @After Annotations

```java
public class CalculatorTest {

    private Calculator mCalculator;

    @Before
    public void setUp() {
        mCalculator = new Calculator();
    }

    @Test
    public void calculator_CorrectAdd_ReturnsTrue() {
        assertEquals(7, mCalculator.add(3, 4),0);
    }

    @Test
    public void calculator_CorrectSub_ReturnsTrue() {
        assertEquals(1, mCalculator.sub(4, 3),0);
    }

    @Test
    public void calculator_CorrectMul_ReturnsTrue() {
        assertEquals(12, mCalculator.mul(3, 4),0);
    }

    @Test
    public void calculator_CorrectDiv_ReturnsTrue() {
        assertEquals(3, mCalculator.div(12, 4),0);
    }

    @After
    public void tearDown() {
        mCalculator = null;
    }
}
```

@Before and @After are called before every test, but if you want to make the setup changes once only before all the tests and once after all the tests then you should use @BeforeClass and @AfterClass. The setUp methods are now setUpBeforeClass rather than setUpBeforeTest. In our @BeforeClass example below setUp and tearDown methods are now declared as public static. The Calculator is be defined as static (see Listing 2-3) so there is now only one instance of the Calculator instead of one for each test.

Listing 2-3. Using @BeforeClass Annotation Instead of @Before

```
private static Calculator mCalculator;

@BeforeClass
public static void setUp() {
    mCalculator = new Calculator();
}
```

HTML Output

JUnit outputs HTML- and XML-style reports in the <path_to_your_project>/app/build/test-results/debug directory. These reports are useful mainly for reference when you're trying to track exactly when a class or classes started to fail or if some package or class has a higher tendency to fail than others (see Figure 2-1).

Figure 2-1. HTML reporting

There is also an XML output in the same directory if you need to import the results into another tool.

Grouping Tests

As your unit tests grow it's not a bad idea to group them as small, medium, or large tests based on how long they're going to take. Writing and executing unit tests should be lightning fast when you're coding, but there may be more comprehensive tests that you might want to run once a day or when the build is checked in.

Figure 2-2 is taken from an old Google testing blog (see `http://googletesting.blogspot.com/2010/12/test-sizes.html`), which does a good job of showing when you should be grouping your tests into medium or large tests so they don't slow down the development process.

Feature	Small	Medium	Large
Network access	No	localhost only	Yes
Database	No	Yes	Yes
File system access	No	Yes	Yes
Use external systems	No	Discouraged	Yes
Multiple threads	No	Yes	Yes
Sleep statements	No	Yes	Yes
System properties	No	Yes	Yes
Time limit (seconds)	60	300	900+

Figure 2-2. Grouping unit tests into categories

Small tests would be normal method-based unit tests with mocked-out database or network access (more on that later). Because Espresso tests need an emulator or device to run, they would automatically be considered medium or large tests.

Listing 2-4 shows the normal way you would annotate whether a test is small or medium with the necessary `import` statements.

Listing 2-4. Classic Unit Testing Grouping

```
import android.test.suitebuilder.annotation.SmallTest;
import android.test.suitebuilder.annotation.MediumTest;

@SmallTest
public void calculator_CorrectAdd_ReturnsTrue() {
    assertEquals(mCalculator.add(3, 4),7,0);
}

@SmallTest
public void calculator_CorrectSub_ReturnsTrue() {
    assertEquals(mCalculator.sub(4, 3),1,0);
}

@MediumTest
public void calculator_CorrectMul_ReturnsTrue() {
    assertEquals(mCalculator.mul(3, 4),12,0);
}

@MediumTest
public void calculator_CorrectDiv_ReturnsTrue() {
    assertEquals(mCalculator.div(12, 4),3,0);
}
```

Parameterized Tests

If we want to test our calculator we're going to have to do a lot more testing than adding, subtracting, multiplying, and dividing combinations of the numbers 3 and 4. Listing 2-5 has a few more tests to give us a little more confidence on our implementation. Run the tests and they all pass.

Listing 2-5. Adding More Test Conditions

```
@Test
public void calculator_CorrectAdd_ReturnsTrue() {
    assertEquals(7, mCalculator.add(3, 4),0);
    assertEquals(7, mCalculator.add(4, 3),0);
    assertEquals(10, mCalculator.add(8, 2),0);
    assertEquals(3, mCalculator.add(-1, 4),0);
    assertEquals(3260, mCalculator.add(3256, 4),0);
}
```

If you're writing unit tests, my guess is you are always looking for ways to write better code and you will think the code in Listing 2-5 smells. All that hard coding doesn't look right, even if it's test code. We can use JUnit's parameterized tests to tidy this up.

Refactor your code to add parameterized tests as follows:

- Add @RunWith(Parameterized.class) at the top of the class to tell the compiler that we are using parameters for our testing

- Add the import statement, import static org.junit. runners.Parameterized.Parameters;

- Create your collections of tests parameters, in this case operandOne, operandTwo, and the expectedResult

- Add the constructor for the class

- Use the parameters to feed your tests

Listing 2-6 shows the complete code. For simplicity's sake, we've converted the code to work only with integers.

Listing 2-6. Paramaterized Testing Example

```
import org.junit.Before;
import org.junit.Test;
import org.junit.runner.RunWith;
import org.junit.runners.Parameterized;


import java.util.Arrays;
import java.util.Collection;

import static org.junit.Assert.assertEquals;
import static org.junit.runners.Parameterized.Parameters;

@RunWith(Parameterized.class)
public class CalculatorParamTest {

    private int mOperandOne;
    private int mOperandTwo;
    private int mExpectedResult;

    private Calculator mCalculator;

    /* Array of tests */
    @Parameters
    public static Collection<Object[]> data() {
        return Arrays.asList(new Object[][] {
                {3, 4, 7},
                {4, 3, 7},
```

```
                {8, 2, 10},
                {-1, 4, 3},
                {3256, 4, 3260}
        });
    }

    /* Constructor */
    public CalculatorParamTest(int mOperandOne, int mOperandTwo, int
    mExpectedResult) {
        this.mOperandOne = mOperandOne;
        this.mOperandTwo = mOperandTwo;
        this.mExpectedResult = mExpectedResult;
    }

    @Before
    public void setUp() {
        mCalculator = new Calculator();
    }

    @Test
    public void testAdd_TwoNumbers() {
        int resultAdd = mCalculator.add(mOperandOne, mOperandTwo);
        assertEquals(resultAdd, mExpectedResult,0);
    }

}
```

When the code runs, we get the following results in the statistics frame (see Figure 2-3).

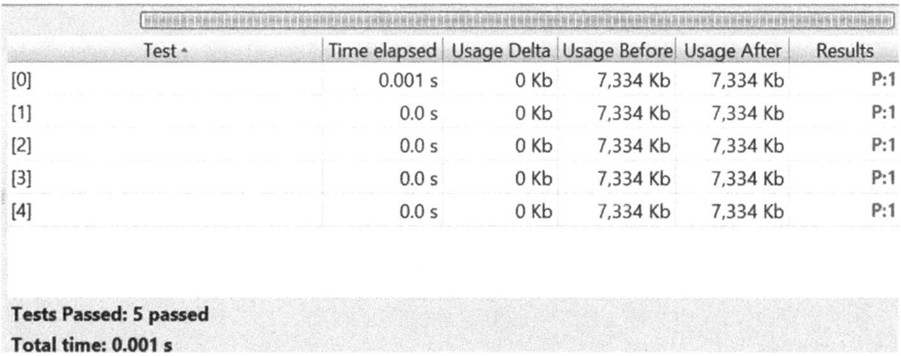

Test ▲	Time elapsed	Usage Delta	Usage Before	Usage After	Results
[0]	0.001 s	0 Kb	7,334 Kb	7,334 Kb	P:1
[1]	0.0 s	0 Kb	7,334 Kb	7,334 Kb	P:1
[2]	0.0 s	0 Kb	7,334 Kb	7,334 Kb	P:1
[3]	0.0 s	0 Kb	7,334 Kb	7,334 Kb	P:1
[4]	0.0 s	0 Kb	7,334 Kb	7,334 Kb	P:1

Tests Passed: 5 passed
Total time: 0.001 s

Figure 2-3. Parameterized test results

Summary

In this chapter we looked at unit tests in more detail. In the next chapter we'll look at some of the third-party tools that you'll want to add to your unit testing tool belt. Later in the book we'll return to unit testing to show how to write unit tests in a TDD (Test Driven Development) environment.

Chapter **3**

Third-Party Tools

JUnit on its own may be all you need, but there are a number of excellent third-party tools that you can bolt onto JUnit that really make your Android testing shine.

In this chapter we'll take a look at the following tools:

- Hamcrest for better assertions

- JaCoCo so we can measure our JUnit code coverage

- Mockito so we can keep our unit tests focused on the code

- Robolectric so we can test our Android activities

- Jenkins for automating our testing

Hamcrest Assertions

Anything more than a simple Hello, World-type application is probably going to need better assertions than those that come with JUnit 4.x. Hamcrest is one option that offers a lot more matchers. It also provides a lot more flexibility by allowing you to now include ranges instead of just single values. As the Hamcrest documentation says, Hamcrest lets you create "Matchers that can be combined to create flexible expressions of intent." Table 3-1 lists most of the Hamcrest assertions available, and you can also write your own.

Table 3-1. Hamcrest Assertions

Package	Assertions
CoreMatchers	allOf, any, anyOf, anything, array, both, containsString, describedAs, either, endsWith, equalTo, everyItem, hasItem, hasItems, instanceOf, is, isA, not, notNullValue, nullValue, sameInstance, startsWith, theInstance
Matchers	allOf, any, anyOf, anything, array, arrayContaining, arrayContainingInAnyOrder, arrayWithSize, both, closeTo, comparesEqualTo, contains, containsInAnyOrder, containsString, describedAs, either, empty, emptyArray, emptyCollectionOf, emptyIterable, emptyIterableOf, endsWith, equalTo, equalToIgnoringCase, equaltToIgnoringWhiteSpace, eventFrom, everyItem, greaterThan, greaterThanOrEqualTo, hasItem, hasItemInArray, hasItems, hasKey, hasProperty, hasSize, hasToString, hasValue, hasXPath, instanceOf, is, isA,isEmptyOrNullString, isIn, isOneOf, iterableWithSize, lessThan, lessThanOrEqualTo, not, notNullValue, nullValue, sameInstance, samePropertyValueAs, startsWith, stringContainsInOrder, theInstance, typeCompatibleWith
Condition	and, matched, matching, notMatched, then
MatcherAssert	assertThat

Listing 3-1 shows how to add the Hamcrest library to your `build.gradle` file to include Hamcrest functionality in your app. Remember to hit the Sync now button.

Listing 3-1. Adding Hamcrest Library Dependency

```
dependencies {
    testCompile 'junit:junit:4.12'
    testCompile 'org.hamcrest:hamcrest-library:1.3'
}
```

Now we refactor our tests so they read more like English (see Listing 3-2).

Listing 3-2. Hamcrest Assertions

```
@Test
public void calculator_CorrectHamAdd_ReturnsTrue() {
    assertThat("Calculator cannot add 3 plus 4", is(7),
    mCalculator.add(3, 4));
}
```

We can also add ranges to our tests using greaterThan and LessThan assertions (see Listing 3-3).

Listing 3-3. greaterThan and lessThan

```
public void calculator_CorrectHamAdd_ReturnsTrue() {
    assertThat("Greater than failed", greaterThan(6), mCalculator.add(3, 4));
    assertThat("Less than failed", lessThan(8), mCalculator.add(3, 4));
}
```

Or, we can combine the two using the both command (see Listing 3-4).

Listing 3-4. Using the both Matcher

```
@Test
public void calculator_CorrectHamAdd_ReturnsTrue() {
    assertThat("Number is out of range", both(greaterThan(6)).
    and(lessThan(8)), mCalculator.add(3, 4),);
}
```

We're only scratching the surface on what you can do with matchers, but no doubt you can see how powerful Hamcrest can make our testing.

JaCoCo

Unit testing needs some form of code coverage to find any untested parts of the code. Code coverage tools output code metric reports and annotated code to show just what code has been unit tested (in green) and what has not been covered by a unit test (in red). Figure 3-1 shows the code coverage figures for JaCoCo which was taken from the eclemma.org web site.

JaCoCo

Element	Missed Instructions	Cov.	Missed Branches	Cov.	Missed	Cxty	Missed	Lines	Missed	Methods	Missed	Classes
org.jacoco.examples		57%		69%	26	55	102	194	22	41	6	12
org.jacoco.agent.rt		82%		89%	32	122	60	308	24	77	7	20
jacoco-maven-plugin		87%		78%	30	142	43	348	5	86	0	17
org.jacoco.core		98%		99%	25	868	34	1,971	19	539	0	85
org.jacoco.report		99%		99%	6	542	5	1,290	2	362	0	65
org.jacoco.ant		98%		99%	5	162	10	428	4	110	0	19
org.jacoco.agent		85%		75%	3	11	5	30	1	7	0	1
Total	1,046 of 19,622	95%	56 of 1,299	96%	127	1,902	259	4,569	77	1,222	13	219

Code Coverage Report for JaCoCo 0.7.6-SNAPSHOT

Figure 3-1. Code coverage example

The code coverage metric measures how much source code has been unit tested. Personally I'm not a huge believer in having a code coverage metric target on an Android project; it should be used as a guide rather than a mandated requirement. However, if a project has 5% code coverage then you're not really doing unit testing and are only paying lip service to the technique.

Android Studio will invoke or call JaCoCo to do the code coverage reports on your unit tests, but you need to perform the following tasks:

- Set `testCoverageEnabled` to true in the `build.gradle` file

- Change the code coverage runner to JaCoCo

- Run unit tests with code coverage

- View the code coverage

To include code coverage in your Android project, set `testCoverageEnabled` to true in your debug `buildTypes` in the `build.gradle` file (see Listing 3-5) and click Sync now after you make the changes.

Listing 3-5. build.gradle JaCoCo Changes

```
buildTypes {
    debug {
        testCoverageEnabled true
    }
}
```

To edit the configurations, go to Run ➤ Edit Configurations (see Figure 3-2).

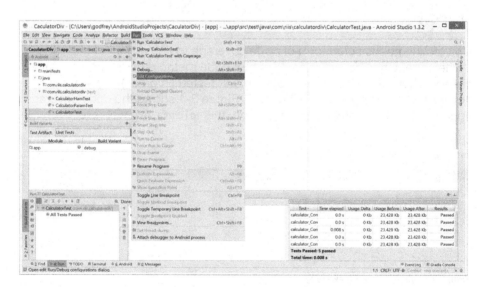

Figure 3-2. Choose Edit Configurations

Click the Code Coverage tab and change the coverage runner to JaCoCo (see Figure 3-3).

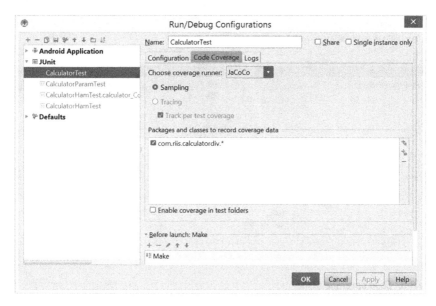

Figure 3-3. *Changing coverage runner*

Run the tests now by right-clicking the method and choosing Run CalculatorTest with Coverage (see Figure 3-4).

Figure 3-4. *Run Calculator Test with Coverage*

The code coverage reports are showing in the Coverage tab (see Figure 3-5), where you can see we have 50% code coverage in our `Calculator` method.

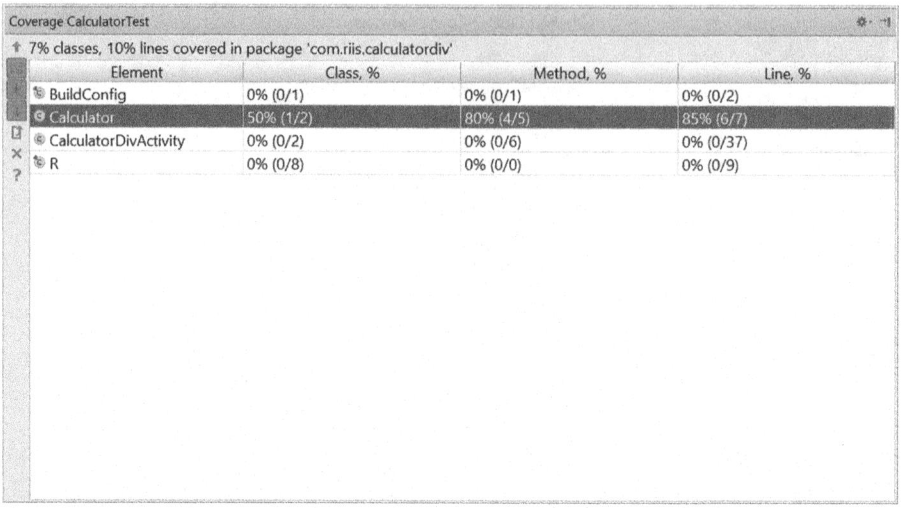

Coverage CalculatorTest				⚙ ⌐
↑ 7% classes, 10% lines covered in package 'com.riis.calculatordiv'				

Element	Class, %	Method, %	Line, %
⬢ BuildConfig	0% (0/1)	0% (0/1)	0% (0/2)
ⓒ Calculator	50% (1/2)	80% (4/5)	85% (6/7)
ⓒ CalculatorDivActivity	0% (0/2)	0% (0/6)	0% (0/37)
⬢ R	0% (0/8)	0% (0/0)	0% (0/9)

Figure 3-5. Code coverage tests

The code coverage red/green is shown in the method, although it can be hard to see (see Figure 3-6). The code coverage integration in Android Studio is new. No doubt, in future versions it will be much easier to see red/green coverage.

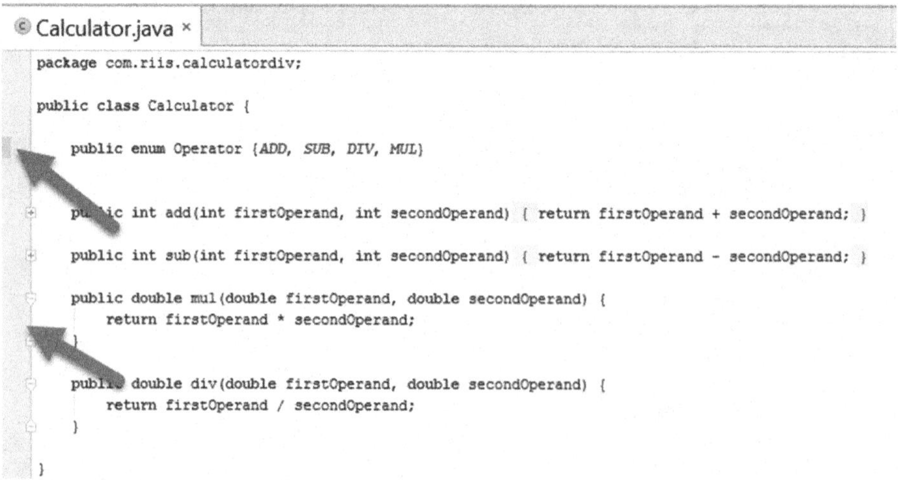

```java
package com.riis.calculatordiv;

public class Calculator {

    public enum Operator {ADD, SUB, DIV, MUL}


    public int add(int firstOperand, int secondOperand) { return firstOperand + secondOperand; }

    public int sub(int firstOperand, int secondOperand) { return firstOperand - secondOperand; }

    public double mul(double firstOperand, double secondOperand) {
        return firstOperand * secondOperand;
    }

    public double div(double firstOperand, double secondOperand) {
        return firstOperand / secondOperand;
    }
}
```

Figure 3-6. Code coverage

Mockito

In Chapter 2, in the section "Grouping Tests," we talked about small, medium, and large tests. In reality, unit tests should always be small tests. But if we're making network connections or reading from the file system or database, then by definition we're not performing small unit tests. We are also making an assumption about a third-party web service or database that may not be running every time we run our tests. So, worst-case scenario, our tests are going to fail, but for the wrong reason (e.g., the network being down). We use mocking frameworks to mock out any code that talks to external resources and get all of our unit tests back to the smaller group. Mockito works very well with Android Studio, so we're going to use that tool in this and subsequent chapters.

Listing 3-6 shows how to add the Mockito library to your build.gradle file by including the testCompile 'org.mockito:mockito-core:1.10.19' library. Once again remember to hit the Sync now link after you're done.

Listing 3-6. Adding Mockito Library

```
dependencies {
    testCompile 'junit:junit:4.12'
    testCompile 'org.hamcrest:hamcrest-library:1.3'
    testCompile 'org.mockito:mockito-core:1.10.19'
}
```

Google's Android sample has a networking app called NetworkConnect which you can find at https://github.com/googlesamples/android-NetworkConnect. Figure 3-7 shows the basic functionality of the app which returns the HTML for the Google web page.

Figure 3-7. NetworkConnect app

Before we mock out the code, we need to cut and paste the network access code into its own class (see Listing 3-7), which we'll call DownloadUrl.

Listing 3-7. DownloadUrl Code

```
public class DownloadUrl {

    public String loadFromNetwork(String urlString) throws IOException {
        InputStream stream = null;
        String str ="";

        try {
            stream = downloadUrl(urlString);
            str = readIt(stream, 88);
        } finally {
```

```
            if (stream != null) {
                stream.close();
            }
        }
        return str;
    }

    public InputStream downloadUrl(String urlString) throws IOException {
        URL url = new URL(urlString);
        HttpURLConnection conn = (HttpURLConnection) url.openConnection();
        conn.setReadTimeout(10000 /* milliseconds */);
        conn.setConnectTimeout(15000 /* milliseconds */);
        conn.setRequestMethod("GET");
        conn.setDoInput(true);
        conn.connect();
        InputStream stream = conn.getInputStream();
        return stream;
    }

    public String readIt(InputStream stream, int len) throws IOException,
    UnsupportedEncodingException {
        Reader reader = null;
        reader = new InputStreamReader(stream, "UTF-8");
        char[] buffer = new char[len];
        reader.read(buffer);
        return new String(buffer);
    }

}
```

The MainActivity now calls DownloadUrl as follows (see Listing 3-8).

Listing 3-8. Updated NetworkConnect MainActivity Code

```
private class DownloadTask extends AsyncTask<String, Void, String> {

    DownloadUrl htmlStr = new DownloadUrl();

    @Override
    protected String doInBackground(String... urls) {
        try {
            return htmlStr.loadFromNetwork(urls[0]);
        } catch (IOException e) {
            return getString(R.string.connection_error);
        }
    }
```

```
/**
 * Uses the logging framework to display the output of the fetch
 * operation in the log fragment.
 */
@Override
protected void onPostExecute(String result) {
  Log.i(TAG, result);
}
}
```

We can now write a unit test to see if the DownloadUrl code is returning HTML in our unit test (see Listing 3-9).

Listing 3-9. Network Connect Unit Test

```
public class DownloadUrlTest {

    DownloadUrl tDownloadUrl;
    String htmlStr;

    @Before
    public void setUp() {
        try {
            htmlStr = tDownloadUrl.loadFromNetwork("http://www.google.com");
        } catch (IOException e) {
            // network error
        }
    }

    @Test
    public void downloadUrlTest_ReturnsTrue() {
            assertThat(htmlStr,containsString("doctype"));
    }
}
```

Because we're making a network call, we should mock out the network access using Mockito. For this example there are only a couple things we need to do to mock out the web server call. First mock out the class so Mockito knows what functionality it needs to replace DownloadUrl tDownloadUrl = Mockito.mock(DownloadUrl.class);. Next, tell Mockito what to return when the method you're testing is called using the Mockito.when().thenReturn() format, which is as follows: Mockito.when(tDownloadUrl.loadFromNetwork("http://www.google.com")). thenReturn("<!doctype html><html itemscope=\"\" itemtype=\"http:// schema.org/WebPage\" lang=\"en\"><head>");.

Now, when the loadFromNetwork call is made it will return our partial web page instead of the actual HTML of www.google.com web page (see Listing 3-10). You can test this by turning your network access on and off.

Listing 3-10. Mocked Network Access

```
@RunWith(MockitoJUnitRunner.class)
public class DownloadUrlTest {

    public DownloadUrl tDownloadUrl = Mockito.mock(DownloadUrl.class);

    @Before
    public void setUp() {
        try {
            Mockito.when(tDownloadUrl.loadFromNetwork("http://
            www.google.com")).thenReturn("<!doctype html><html
            itemscope=\"\" itemtype=\"http://schema.org/WebPage\"
            lang=\"en\"><head>");
        } catch (IOException e) {
            // network error
        }
    }

    @Test
    public void downloadUrlTest_ReturnsTrue() {
        try {
            assertThat(tDownloadUrl.loadFromNetwork("http://www.google.com"),
            containsString("doctype"));
        } catch (IOException e) {
            //
        }
    }
}
```

We will return to Mockito in the next chapter and show you how to mock out database and shared preferences access as well as how to use other tools to extend the Mockito functionality to help decouple or separate out your code.

Robolectric

You can't test Android apps unless you test Android activities. You can test around it using tools like Mockito and JUnit but you're missing a key element of your app if you're not testing its activities. You can't be sure that your app is displaying the correct information if you don't test what the activities are displaying to your users. This is relatively easy to using an emulator testing framework such as Espresso or Calabash. But we can also test it without an emulator if we use Robolectric.

To install Robolectric 3.0 add the following dependency to your build.gradle file (see Listing 3-11).

Listing 3-11. Adding Robolectric Library Dependency

```
dependencies {
    testCompile 'junit:junit:4.12'
    testCompile 'org.robolectric:robolectric:3.0'
}
```

You will also need to make a change to your App configuration. Go to Run-Edit Configurations and if you're running on a Mac or Linux then change the Working Directory to $MODULE_DIR$ or if you're running on a Windows machine add a \app to the end of the Working Directory (see Figure 3-8).

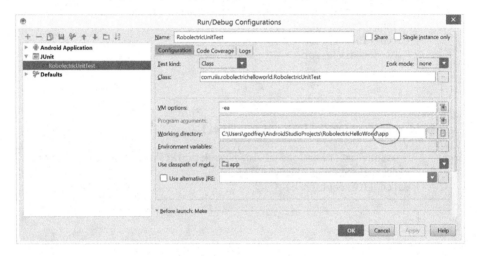

Figure 3-8. Robolectric Working Directory fix

Listing 3-12 shows a unit test that uses Robolectric to test that Hello World is displayed on the `MainActivity`. Note the configuration information which sets the target SDK to API 21 and tells Robolectric where to find the `AndroidManifest.xml` file.

Listing 3-12. Robolectric Hello World

```
@RunWith(RobolectricGradleTestRunner.class)
@Config(constants = BuildConfig.class, sdk = 21, manifest = "src/main/
AndroidManifest.xml")
public class RobolectricUnitTest {
    @Test
    public void shouldHaveHappySmiles() throws Exception {
        String hello = new MainActivity().getResources().getString(R.string.
        hello_world);
        assertThat(hello, equalTo("Hello world!"));
    }
}
```

Run the test in the same way you would run unit tests by right clicking on the test class name and choosing 'Run RobolectricTest'. The test passes without the need for an emulator. Relatively speaking Robolectric tests take longer than JUnit4 tests but they are still considerably faster than emulator tests.

Figure 3-9. Robolectric Hello World test passes

Jenkins

Moving to an Agile process can create considerable overhead. Thankfully we no longer have to worry about the emulator taking so long to fire up for vanilla JUnit tests. It takes seconds now instead of minutes. However, as the app grows and the corresponding number of unit tests grows too, then eventually it's going to take time to run the tests manually. The number of steps to build and test the apps correctly will also start to become more complex. And as humans are not good at tedious multistep processes, it makes sense to use a Continuous Integration (CI) server to automate the process wherever possible to reduce any unnecessary testing errors.

For our purposes we're going to use Jenkins because it has so many plug-ins available. However, there are many other options, such as Travis, TeamCity, or Bamboo, that can work equally well if you're more familiar with those CI environments.

Install

Download the Jenkins server from `http://jenkins-ci.org/`. Install it and go to `http://localhost:8080` and you should see the screen shown in Figure 3-10.

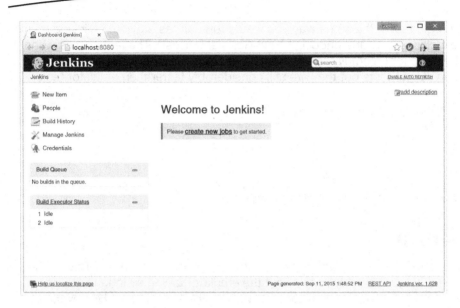

Figure 3-10. Jenkins start-up screen

Configure Jenkins

To make it useful in our Android environment we're going to need to add a number of plug-ins. Click on Manage Jenkins ➤ Manage Plugins (see Figure 3-10) and search for and add the Gradle and GIT plug-in or whatever other source code management system you use. When you're done, your installed plug-ins screen should look something like the screen in Figure 3-11.

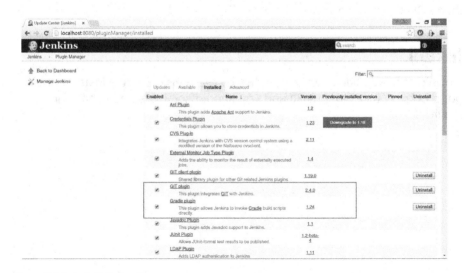

Figure 3-11. Installed plug-ins

Next we need to configure Jenkins so it knows where you installed Android. Click Manage Jenkins ➤ Configure System, scroll down to Global Properties, click Environment variables check box, and enter the directory for the ANDROID_HOME where you installed Android (see Figure 3-12).

Global properties

☑ Environment variables
List of key-value pairs

| name | ANDROID_HOME |
| value | c:\android\sdk |

Delete

Figure 3-12. Setting Environment variables

Create Automated job

Now that we've configured Jenkins we need to create our first automated job. Go back to the dashboard and click create new jobs (Figure 3-10). Enter the name of your project and choose Freestyle project (see Figure 3-13).

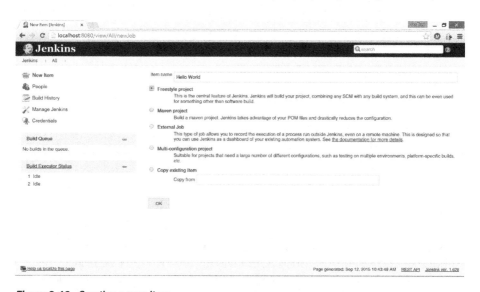

Figure 3-13. Creating a new item

We need to tell Jenkins where to find the code. In this example we're using Git as our source code management system. Here we're again using the Google NetworkConnect sample. Enter the Git repository URL. As it's a public repo there are no credentials, so we're going to skip that. There is also only one branch, so we can leave the Branch Specifier as master (see Figure 3-14).

Source Code Management

- ○ None
- ○ CVS
- ○ CVS Projectset
- ◉ Git

Repositories

Repository URL   https://github.com/googlesamples/android-NetworkConnect/

Credentials   - none - ▾   ← Add

Advanced...

Add Repository   Delete Repository

Branches to build   Branch Specifier (blank for 'any')   */master

Add Branch   Delete Branch

Figure 3-14. Enter Network Connect repository details

Scroll down to the Build section and choose Invoke Gradle script
(see Figure 3-15).

Build

Add build step   ▾

Execute Windows batch command

Execute shell

Invoke Ant

Invoke Gradle script

Invoke top-level Maven targets

Figure 3-15. Invoke Gradle script

In the Build step choose Use Gradle Wrapper, check Make gradlew
executable and From Root Build Script Dir. Enter --refresh-dependencies
and --profile in the switches section. And in this case enter assemble in
the Tasks section. Click save (see Figure 3-16).

Build

Invoke Gradle script

○ Invoke Gradle
◉ Use Gradle Wrapper
  Make gradlew executable ☑
  From Root Build Script Dir ☑

Build step description

Switches   --refresh-dependencies --profile

Tasks   assemble

Root Build script

Build File

Specify Gradle build file to run. Also, some environment variables are available to the build script

Force GRADLE_USER_HOME to use workspace ☐

Figure 3-16. Configure the Build

Now we're ready to build our app. Click Build Now on the Project page (see Figure 3-17).

Figure 3-17. Project page

Once the Build starts, you'll see a progress indicator to see how your task is doing. If you want to see what's happening then click the Build Number (see Figure 3-18).

Figure 3-18. View Build progress

Now click Console Output and you can see what's happening as if you were running the app from the command line (see Figure 3-19).

Figure 3-19. Click Console Output

In our example there are no errors and the Build is successful (see Figure 3-20). If that's not the case, then the Console Output page can be really helpful to see what failed.

Figure 3-20. Console Output

We'll be using Jenkins later in the book to automate our JUnit and Espresso tests.

Summary

In this chapter we've looked at a number of tools that we're going to use throughout the book to make our testing more effective and more efficient. In the recent past it's been a very frustrating task to get this stack up and running, but thankfully that is no longer the case.

Chapter 4

Mocking

One of the major goals whether it's on the Android platform or not is to isolate the code that we're testing. When we write our tests, we want to test a specific class's method without any of the associated interactions with other classes in the app or any external elements, such as a web service. We should be testing a single method, not its dependencies and this method should be the only code covered by the test with everything else mocked.

Mocking out these third-party interactions is a great way to help us put a fence around a method so we're not reliant on such things as the network or a device's location or US or UK time when we're doing our testing. The only reason a test should fail is because there's something wrong with the code, never because external dependencies (like the wifi) are not working.

But there's another major Android-specific reason we want to use Mocking frameworks and that's because we want all our tests to be @SmallTests, tests that can be run without an emulator. Mocking dependencies allows you to get your tests to run orders of magnitude quicker than the dreaded alternative, which is to wait a couple minutes for the emulator to start. Sure there are times when you need to use an emulator, such as when you're testing Activities (see Chapter 5), but if you're not testing Activities mocking gives you the confidence to annotate your tests as @SmallTest without the emulator overhead.

In this chapter we'll look at using Mockito to mock out the following interactions for both test isolation and faster test execution.

- Shared preferences
- Time
- Settings
- SQLite databases

We've also already covered web services briefly in Chapter 2.

Shared Preferences

Shared preferences are typically stored as xml files on the device in the
/data/data/<name of your package> folder. Under normal circumstances,
any testing that requires file system access means using an emulator, unless
we use Mockito.

In our example, to show how this works, we're going to use a simple
login app. It doesn't do much other than let you log in with a username,
password, and e-mail address and then display the information on the
second page (see Figure 4-1).

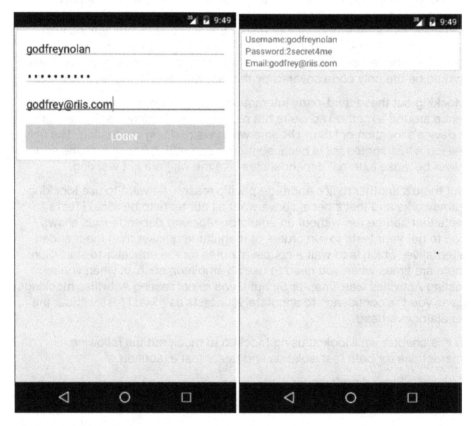

Figure 4-1. Registration app

In our fake app we want to show that the user has already registered, so the first time the user logs in we're going to write to the app's shared preferences. Listing 4-1 shows the code for writing to the shared preferences file. The method takes an Activity and a string as its parameters. The complete code is available in the Source Code/Download area of the Apress web site the Source Code/Download area of the Apress web site (www.apress.com).

Listing 4-1. Saving to the Shared Preferences

```
public void saveSharedPreferences(Activity activity, String spValue) {
    SharedPreferences preferences = activity.getPreferences(Activity.MODE_
    PRIVATE);
    preferences.edit().putString(SHAREDPREF, spValue).apply();
}
```

Listing 4-2 shows the call to check to see the value stored in our shared preferences.

Listing 4-2. Reading from Shared Preferences

```
public String getSharedPreferences(Activity activity) {
    SharedPreferences preferences = activity
            .getPreferences(Activity.MODE_PRIVATE);
    return preferences.getString(SHAREDPREF, "Not registered");
}
```

Run the app on the Android emulator and enter your login credentials. You can see what's stored in the shared preferences, by running the adb shell command on the emulator (see Listing 4-3). It will also work on a rooted device.

Listing 4-3. Login App's Shared Preference

```
>adb shell
root@generic:/ # cd /data/data/com.riis.hellopreferences/shared_prefs
root@generic:/data/data/com.riis.hellopreferences/shared_prefs # ls
MainActivity.xml
root@generic:/data/data/com.riis.hellopreferences/shared_prefs # cat
MainActivity.xml
<?xml version='1.0' encoding='utf-8' standalone='yes' ?>
<map>
    <string name="registered">true</string>
</map>
```

Shared preferences is built into Android functionality, meaning that we don't need to test it. In a real app we may want to test our code, assuming that the user is already registered when the app is under test. Listing 4-4 shows the mocked-out call for the getSharedPreferences method, sharedPreferencesTest_ReturnsTrue.

Listing 4-4. Mocked getSharedPreferences

```
// Annotation to tell compiler we're using Mockito
@RunWith(MockitoJUnitRunner.class)
public class UserPreferencesTest {

    // Use Mockito to initialize UserPreferences
    public UserPreferences tUserPreferences = Mockito.mock(UserPreferences.
    class);

    private Activity tActivity;

    @Before
    public void setUp() {
        // setup the test infrastructure
        // Use Mockito to declare the return value of getSharedPreferences()
        Mockito.when(tUserPreferences.getSharedPreferences(tActivity)).
        thenReturn("true");
    }

    @Test
    public void sharedPreferencesTest_ReturnsTrue() {
        // Perform test
        Assert.assertThat(tUserPreferences.getSharedPreferences(tActivity),
        is("true"));
    }
}
```

sharedPreferencesTest_ReturnsTrue always returns true so we can bypass the shared preferences and get on with what's important in our testing. In this example we fix the shared preferences code so that it always returns true. Mainly because it never actually runs the shared preferences code. The setup block tells Mockito how you want it to behave, and the mocked version of that class will behave as it was instructed, always returning true.

Time

Taking advantage of interfaces can be a very useful mocking technique. For example, if we have a Clock interface that calls a Clock implementation class which tells the time, then we use Mockito to mock the interface Clock class to provide our own Android date/time environment. The interface abstraction allows us to hide the implementation so we can have complete control over time zones and time of day and create a lot more edge case tests to really work our code. This is a simple example of "coding to the interface". The interface is the contract we're trying to satisfy when we write our code. However when testing the implementation the interface can talk to either the real implementation, the mocked one, or even a combination of the two.

Listing 4-5 shows the Clock interface code.

Listing 4-5. Clock Interface

```
import java.util.Date;

public interface Clock {
    Date getDate();
}
```

Listing 4-6 shows the Clock implementation code.

Listing 4-6. ClockImpl Code

```
import java.util.Date;

public class ClockImpl implements Clock {
    @Override
    public Date getDate() {
        return new Date();
    }
}
```

The concept here is just like the Shared Preferences. We don't have to test any java.util.Date functionality; we want to test only the code we write that uses it. Listing 4-7 has a couple of simple methods that double and triple the time in milliseconds.

Listing 4-7. Timechange Code

```
public class TimeChange {

    private final Clock dateTime;

    public TimeChange(final Clock dateTime) {
        this.dateTime = dateTime;
    }

    public long getDoubleTime(){
        return dateTime.getDate().getTime()*2;
    }
```

```
    public long getTripleTime(){
        return dateTime.getDate().getTime()*3;
    }
}
```

In our testing code (see Listing 4-8), we mock out the Clock and the java.util.Date classes which allows us to set the time to whatever value we want and run some assertions to make sure our doubleTime and tripleTime methods are behaving as expected.

Listing 4-8. TimeChangeTest Code

```
// Tell Android we're using Mockito
@RunWith(MockitoJUnitRunner.class)
public class TimeChangeTest {

    private TimeChange timeChangeTest;

    @Before
    public void setUp() {
        // Mock the Date class
        final Date date = Mockito.mock(Date.class);
        Mockito.when(date.getTime()).thenReturn(10L);

        // Mock the Clock class interface final Clock dt =
        Mockito.mock(Clock.class);
        Mockito.when(dt.getDate()).thenReturn(date);

        timeChangeTest = new TimeChange(dt);
    }

    @Test
    public void timeTest() {
        final long doubleTime = timeChangeTest.getDoubleTime();
        final long tripleTime = timeChangeTest.getTripleTime();
        assertEquals(20, doubleTime);
        assertEquals(30, tripleTime);
    }
}
```

System Properties

If we want to avoid using the emulator for testing we need to fake any Java or built-in Android functionality. In most cases this is exactly what we're looking for; as we've seen in the previous example, we're not testing the shared preferences functionality or the date functionality. Similarly, we don't want to test Android settings (such as the Audio Manager).

Our AudioHelper code has a single method, maximizeVolume. Listing 4-9 shows our code to max out the volume.

Listing 4-9. Testing the Max-Min Limits of Our Code

```
import android.media.AudioManager;

public class AudioHelper {
    public void maximizeVolume(AudioManager audioManager) {
        int max = audioManager.getStreamMaxVolume(AudioManager.STREAM_RING);
        audioManager.setStreamVolume(AudioManager.STREAM_RING, max, 0);
    }
}
```

Listing 4-10 shows our test code to set the ringer to the max volume.

Listing 4-10. Max Volume Limits

```
/**
 * Unit tests for the AudioManager logic.
 */
// Define the test as SmallTest for grouping tests
@SmallTest
public class AudioHelperTest {
    private final int MAX_VOLUME = 100;

    @Test
    public void maximizeVolume_Maximizes_Volume() {
        // Create a mockAudioManager object using Mockito
        AudioManager audioManager = Mockito.mock(AudioManager.class);

        // Inform Mockito what to return when audioManager.
        getStreamMaxVolume is called Mockito.when(audioManager.
        getStreamMaxVolume(AudioManager.STREAM_RING)).thenReturn
        (MAX_VOLUME);
        // Run method we're testing, passing mock AudioManager
        new AudioHelper().maximizeVolume(audioManager);

        //verify with Mockito that setStreamVolume to 100 was called.
        Mockito.verify(audioManager).setStreamVolume (AudioManager.STREAM_
        RING, MAX_VOLUME, 0);
    }
}
```

We create the mock AudioManager object, and tell our test code to return the MaxVolume when we make the call and then we verify that the Mockito set the volume to our max when the call was made.

Database

Shared preferences are great for storing parameters, URLs (uniform resource locators), or API (application programming interface) keys to third-party libraries, but they are not so good for large amounts of tabular data. If you have a lot of spreadsheet-type data in Android that you want to keep on the phone, then it's more common to use a SQLite database for storage as it's free, lightweight, and does a great job with 10s to 1,000s of rows of data. If you need to upgrade to bigger data sets, then you're much more likely to store them on a back-end server than on the device itself.

Using our sample app (see Figure 4-1, again), we can add the username and e-mail to a SQLite database. To write to the SQLite database you need SQLHelper code (see Listing 4-11). This is typical boilerplate code used for Android SQLite applications. It creates and upgrades the database and its tables. In this case the Users table has a column for an autogenerated ID as well as the user's name and e-mail address.

Listing 4-11. SQLite Code to Create User Database

```java
public class SQLHelper extends SQLiteOpenHelper {
    private static final int DATABASE_VERSION = 1;
    private static final String DATABASE_NAME = "UserDb";

    private static final String TABLE_USERS = "Users";
    private static final String KEY_ID = "id";
    private static final String KEY_FIRST_NAME = "firstName";
    private static final String KEY_LAST_NAME = "lastName";

    private static final String[] COLUMNS = {KEY_ID, KEY_FIRST_NAME,
    KEY_LAST_NAME};

    public SQLHelper(Context context) {
        super(context, DATABASE_NAME, null, DATABASE_VERSION);
    }

    @Override
    public void onCreate(SQLiteDatabase db) {
        String CREATE_USER_TABLE = "CREATE TABLE Users ( " +
                "id INTEGER PRIMARY KEY AUTOINCREMENT, " +
                "firstName TEXT, "+
                "lastName TEXT )";
        db.execSQL(CREATE_USER_TABLE);
    }
}
```

```
@Override
public void onUpgrade(SQLiteDatabase db, int oldVersion, int newVersion) {
    db.execSQL("DROP TABLE IF EXISTS Users");
    this.onCreate(db);
}

public void addUser(User user){
    SQLiteDatabase db = this.getWritableDatabase();

    ContentValues values = new ContentValues();
    values.put(KEY_FIRST_NAME, user.getFirstName());
    values.put(KEY_LAST_NAME, user.getLastName());

    db.insert(TABLE_USERS, null, values);
    db.close();
}

public User getUser(int id){
    SQLiteDatabase db = this.getReadableDatabase();
    Cursor cursor = db.query(TABLE_USERS, COLUMNS, " id = ?", new
    String[] { String.valueOf(id) }, null, null, null, null);

    if (cursor != null) {
        cursor.moveToFirst();
    }

    User user = new User();
    user.setId(Integer.parseInt(cursor.getString(0)));
    user.setFirstName(cursor.getString(1));
    user.setLastName(cursor.getString(2));
    return user;
}
}
}
```

In the past, developers have isolated their databases during testing by using an in-memory SQLite database. You can do this by leaving the DATABASE_ NAME as null (i.e., super(context, null, null, DATABASE_VERSION);). Unfortunately, this won't work for us as it still requires an emulator, so we're going to have to rely on our mocking.

Listing 4-12 shows the UserOperations code that we want to test: this is our create, read, update, delete (CRUD) code.

Listing 4-12. CRUD Code for Our Database Calls

```
public class UserOperations {

    private DataBaseWrapper dbHelper;
    private String[] USER_TABLE_COLUMNS = { DataBaseWrapper.USER_ID,
    DataBaseWrapper.USER_NAME, DataBaseWrapper.USER_EMAIL };
    private SQLiteDatabase database;

    public UserOperations(Context context) {
        dbHelper = new DataBaseWrapper(context);
    }

    public void open() throws SQLException {
        database = dbHelper.getWritableDatabase();
    }

    public void close() {
        dbHelper.close();
    }

    public User addUser(String name, String email) {

        ContentValues values = new ContentValues();
        values.put(DataBaseWrapper.USER_NAME, name);
        values.put(DataBaseWrapper.USER_EMAIL, email);

        long userId = database.insert(DataBaseWrapper.USERS, null, values);

        Cursor cursor = database.query(DataBaseWrapper.USERS,
                USER_TABLE_COLUMNS, DataBaseWrapper.USER_ID + " = "
                        + userId, null, null, null, null);

        cursor.moveToFirst();

    }

    public void deleteUser(User comment) {
        long id = comment.getId();

        database.delete(DataBaseWrapper.USERS, DataBaseWrapper.USER_ID
                + " = " + id, null);
    }

    public List getAllUsers() {
        List users = new ArrayList();

        Cursor cursor = database.query(DataBaseWrapper.USERS,
                USER_TABLE_COLUMNS, null, null, null, null, null);
```

```
            cursor.moveToFirst();
            while (!cursor.isAfterLast()) {
                User user = parseUser(cursor);
                users.add(user);
                cursor.moveToNext();
            }

            cursor.close();
            return users;
        }

    public String getUserEmailById(long id) {

        User regUser = null;

        String sql = "SELECT " + DataBaseWrapper.USER_EMAIL + " FROM " +
        DataBaseWrapper.USERS + " WHERE " + DataBaseWrapper.USER_ID + " = ?";

        Cursor cursor = database.rawQuery(sql, new String[] { id + "" });

        if (cursor.moveToNext()) {
            return cursor.getString(0);
        } else {
            return "N/A";
        }

    }

    private User parseUser(Cursor cursor) {
        User user = new User();
        user.setId((cursor.getInt(0)));
        user.setName(cursor.getString(1));
        return user;
    }

}
```

In our tests we're going to mock out an addUser(name, email) call
(see Listing 4-13).

Listing 4-13. testMockUser Code

```
/**
 * Unit tests for the User Database class.
 */
@SmallTest
public class DatabaseTest {
    private User joeSmith = new User("Joe", "Smith");
    private final int USER_ID = 1;
```

```
@Test
public void testMockUser() {
    //mock SQLHelper
    SQLHelper dbHelper = Mockito.mock(SQLHelper.class);
    //have mockito return joeSmith when calling dbHelper getUser
    Mockito.when(dbHelper.getUser(USER_ID)).thenReturn(joeSmith);

    //Assert joeSmith is returned by getUser
    assertEquals(dbHelper.getUser(USER_ID), joeSmith);
    }
}
```

In the setup we mock out the dbHelper class as well as the underlying
SQLiteDatabase. In testMockUser we do a simple test call that the returned
user is Joe Smith.

Jenkins

In an ideal environment, we want to have the tests run automatically, every
time the code is checked in using a Continuous Integration Server such as
Jenkins, which we covered in Chapter 3.

To run the unit tests in Jenkins, click Add Build Step ➤ Invoke Gradle script
and add the testCompile task as shown in Figure 4-2.

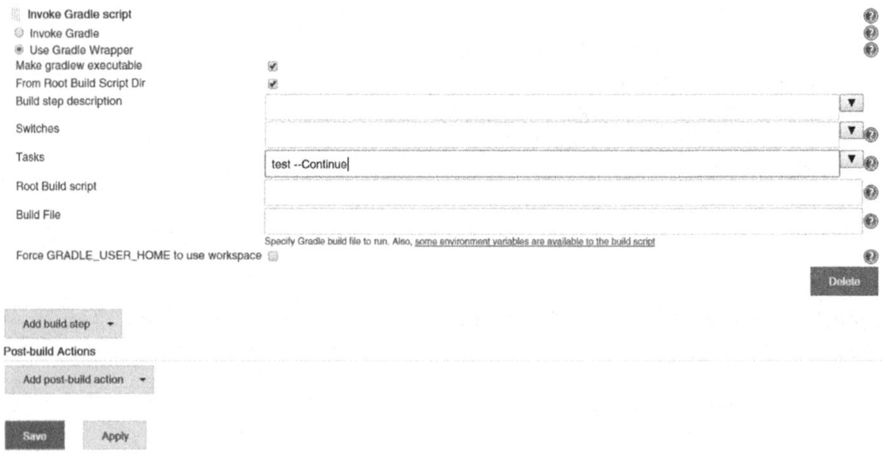

Figure 4-2. Running unit tests in Jenkins

Summary

In this chapter we've looked at a number of scenarios for using Mockito to isolate our tests from any underlying Android and Java dependencies. The reason we do this is to ensure that we are only testing the code we wish to test, and not any of the code interacting with it. The code you write should all be unit tested, including mocks to mimic the interactions with its dependencies.

Working code from this chapter can be found online on the Apress website.

Chapter 5

Espresso

Android apps fail for a number of reasons other than simple logic errors. At its most basic, the app may not install correctly, or there may be a problem when you move from landscape to portrait and back again. Because of fragmentation, the layout might not work on any number of devices that you haven't had the time to test it on, or it could hang if the network is down.

It's just not possible to test for these conditions using unit testing. We're going to have to use another testing tool to test our GUIs (graphical user interfaces) or activities. And, unfortunately, it also means we're back to using devices and emulators to do our testing.

There are lots of options out there, such as UIAutomator, Calabash, Robotium, and Selenium. Until recently I've been using Calabash because of its Given/When/Then writing format which works great with business users. However, there are significant advantages to using Espresso, which are too hard to resist.

All these other products are third-party products whereas Espresso is a Google first-party product. Usually this wouldn't be any sort of advantage, but because of Espresso's ability to hook into the Android life cycle it does a wonderful job of knowing exactly when the activity is ready to perform your tests. GUI tests in Android are typically full of `sleep()` commands to ensure that the activity is ready to accept your data. With Espresso there is simply no need for any waiting or sleeping; it just fires the test when the app is ready to accept the input data. This synchronization between the UI thread and Espresso means that tests run much more reliably than with the other tools. If a test fails, then it's because there's an error in your code rather than that you need to add more time to the `sleep()` command.

onView

While we already looked at the Espresso in Chapter 1, it makes sense to go back to basics and do a real Hello, World Espresso test.

In Chapter 1 we showed how to set up the Espresso environment as follows:

- Prerequisites: Install the Android Support Repository
- Add Espresso dependency in `build.gradle` (app) file
- Choose Android Test Instrumentation test artifact in Build Variant
- Create GUI tests in `src/androidTest/java` folder
- Right-click tests to run tests

Instead of JUnit or Hamcrest matchers and assertions, Espresso uses the OnView format. This has three parts, namely a ViewMatcher to find the element in the activity we're testing, a ViewAction to perform the action (e.g., click) and finally a ViewAssertion to make sure the text matches and the test passes.

```
onView(ViewMatcher)
      .perform(ViewAction)
      .check(ViewAssertion);
```

Hello World

Listing 5-1 shows the code for the standard Android Hello World app.

Listing 5-1. Hello World

```
public class MainActivity extends Activity {

    private TextView mLabel;

    @Override
    protected void onCreate(Bundle savedInstanceState) {
        super.onCreate(savedInstanceState);
        setContentView(R.layout.activity_main);

    }
}
```

Figure 5-1 shows the app running on the emulator. Our simple Espresso test is going to find the text and make sure it's really saying Hello world!

Figure 5-1. Hello world!

Listing 5-2 shows the code for the simple test. The test is annotated as a @ LargeTest because we need the emulator to run Espresso tests. We're using a JUnit4 rule to launch Main Activity (see the @Rule annotation).

Once we have access to the activity, we use the onView code to find our Hello World text and a .check to see if the text is what it was defined as in the strings.xml file. In this case there is no need for the .perform step, so it is omitted.

Listing 5-2. Hello World Espresso Test

```
@RunWith(AndroidJUnit4.class)
@LargeTest
public class MainActivityTest {

    @Rule
    public ActivityTestRule<MainActivity> activityTestRule
            = new ActivityTestRule<>(MainActivity.class);
```

```
@Test
public void helloWorldTest() {
    onView(withId(R.id.hello_world))
        .check(matches(withText(R.string.hello_world)));

    }
}
```

The test passes and the results are shown in Android Studio similar to the unit test output (see Figure 5-2).

Figure 5-2. Hello World Espresso test results

Adding Buttons

Next let's add a button to our Hello World code. We do this by adding the code in Listing 5-3 to our `activity_main.xml` file. The `button_label` string will also need to be added to the `strings.xml` file. Note that the button is enabled by default.

Listing 5-3. Adding Hello World Button

```
<Button
    android:id="@+id/button"
    android:text="@string/button_label"
    android:layout_width="wrap_content"
    android:layout_height="wrap_content" />
```

Figure 5-3 shows our modified app with the new button.

Figure 5-3. Hello World with button

We want to make sure the button is on or enabled. Listing 5-4 now shows the test code. This time we're using the .perform action to click the button.

Listing 5-4. onView Button Test

```
@Test
public void helloWorldButtonTest(){
    onView(withId(R.id.button))
            .perform(click())
            .check(matches(isEnabled()));
}
```

The test successfully runs as everything is green (see Figure 5-4).

Figure 5-4. Hello World test results

ViewMatchers

Table 5-1 shows the available ViewMatcher options.

Table 5-1. ViewMatcher

Category	Matcher
User Properties	withId, withText, withTagKey, withTagValue, hasContentDescription, withContentDescription, withHint, withSpinnerText, hasLinks, hasEllipsizedText, hasMultilineTest
UI Properties	isDisplayed, isCompletelyDisplayed, isEnabled, hasFocus, isClickable, isChecked, isNotChecked, withEffectiveVisibility, isSelected
ObjectMatcher	allOf, anyOf, is, not, endsWith, startsWith, instanceOf
Hierarchy	withParent, withChild, hasDescendant, isDescendantOfA, hasSibling, isRoot
Input	supportsInputMethods, hasIMEAction
Class	isAssignableFrom, withClassName
Root Matchers	isFocusable, isTouchable, isDialog, withDecorView, isPlatformPopup

ViewActions

Table 5-2 shows the available ViewAction options.

Table 5-2. ViewAction

Category	Action
Click/Press	click, doubleClick, longClick, pressBack, pressIMEActionButton, pressKey, pressMenuKey, closeSoftKeyboard, openLink
Gestures	scrollTo, swipeLeft, swipeRight, swipeUp, swipeDown
Text	clearText, typeText, typeTextIntoFocusedView, replaceText

ViewAssertions

Table 5-3 shows the available ViewAssertion options.

Table 5-3. ViewAssertion

Package	Assertions
Layout Assertions	noEllipsizedText, noMultilineButtons, noOverlaps
Position Assertions	isLeftOf, isRightOf, isLeftAllginedWith, isRightAlignedWith, isAbove, isBelow, isBottomAlignedWith, isTopAlignedWith
Other	matches, doesNotExist, selectedDescendentsMatch

onData

onView won't be able to find the data when we're using any AdapterViews such as ListView, GridView, or Spinner. For AdapterViews we have to use onData in conjunction with the onView to locate and test the item.

The onData format is as follows:

```
onData(ObjectMatcher)
  .DataOptions
  .perform(ViewAction)
  .check(ViewAssertion)
```

The DataOptions available are inAdapterView, atPosition, or onChildView.

To Do List

To see how this works let's look at how to test the ToDoList application which has a ListView adapter (see Figure 5-5).

Figure 5-5. ToDoList application

Our application uses a ListView adapter. Listing 5-5 shows the code.

Listing 5-5. To Do List Code

```java
public class MainActivity extends Activity {

    private TextView mtxtSelectedItem;

    @Override
    protected void onCreate(Bundle savedInstanceState) {
        super.onCreate(savedInstanceState);
        setContentView(R.layout.activity_main);

        mtxtSelectedItem = (TextView) findViewById(R.id.txt_selected_item);

        String[] todolist = {"pick up the kids","pay bills","do laundry",
                             "buy groceries ","go the gym","clean
                             room","call mum"};
```

```
        List<String> list = Arrays.asList(todolist);
        ArrayAdapter<String> adapter =
                            new ArrayAdapter(this, android.R.layout.
                        ·   simple_list_item_1, list);
        ListView listView = (ListView) findViewById(R.id.list_of_todos);
        listView.setAdapter(adapter);
        listView.setOnItemClickListener(new AdapterView.
        OnItemClickListener() {
            @Override
            public void onItemClick(AdapterView<?> parent, View view, int
            position, long id) {
                String text = ((TextView) view).getText().toString();
                Toast.makeText(getApplicationContext(), text, Toast.LENGTH_
                LONG).show();
                mtxtSelectedItem.setText(text);
            }
        });
    }

}
```

A simple test to make sure everything is working okay would be to pick
something on the todo list, such as "go to the gym." Listing 6-6 shows
the Espresso code. We're telling the test to look at position [4] in the
AdapterView in the onData code and then passing that to the onView so that
it can check that the text does indeed say "go to the gym."

Listing 5-6. onData Test Code

```
@RunWith(AndroidJUnit4.class)
@LargeTest
public class MainActivityTest {

    @Rule
    public ActivityTestRule<MainActivity> activityTestRule
            = new ActivityTestRule<>(MainActivity.class);

    @Test
    public void toDoListTest(){
        onData(anything())
                .inAdapterView(withId(R.id.list_of_todos)).atPosition(4)
                .perform(click());

        onView(withId(R.id.txt_selected_item))
                .check(matches(withText("go to the gym")));
    }

}
```

Run the test once again using the emulator or on a device.

Jenkins

To run the Espresso tests in Jenkins, click Add Build Step ➤ Invoke Gradle Script and add the connectedCheck task (see Figure 5-6).

Figure 5-6. Adding Espresso tests in Jenkins

Espresso needs an emulator to perform its tests, so you also need to install the Android Emulator plug-in. You can choose to let Jenkins use an existing emulator or create a new one (see Figure 5-7).

Figure 5-7. Using an existing emulator

Summary

In this chapter we've looked at a number of Espresso tests using both onView and onData. Finally, if you're wondering how many Espresso tests we should have in our suite of tests, then go back to our Agile Test Pyramid in Chapter 1 (Figure 1-1) and you will see that we should always have a lot more unit tests than Espresso tests, or to put it another way more @SmallTests than @LargeTests.

Chapter 6

Test-Driven Development

It wouldn't be right if we didn't make an effort to show test-driven development (TDD) in action. So, in this chapter we're going to create an app from scratch using our TDD approach. Using TDD, we're going to create a sample app for a daily horoscope. I'm not an astrology fanatic by any means, but it's a simple enough app that will allow us to show our TDD techniques in action.

Understanding Test-Driven Development

TDD means that we take the first feature on our list of features and code using the following process:

- Write a test first and see it fail (red)
- Implement the simplest possible solution to get our test to pass (green)
- Refactor to remove any code smells (refactor)

In reality you're probably going to need more than a single test to satisfy a feature. But once you're happy that you've implemented the feature, take another feature from the list and repeat the red/green/refactor process until all the features are completed.

> **Note**   In classic TDD, whether it's in Java, C++ or C#, you don't have to worry
> about any infrastructure. But things aren't that straightforward in Android. When
> you create a Java class to test, you often have to create an Activity that will
> display or interact with that Java class. So, when you say write the simplest
> possible solution to get the unit test to pass, that will also have to include some
> Android Activity code too. Alternatively, you can leave that to the refactoring
> stage if you like, but it just needs to be completed somewhere in the red/green/
> refactor process.

Unit Testing and TDD

So far we've been focused on unit testing our Android apps. But unit testing
is not necessarily TDD. Test-driven development means writing the unit test
before writing the code, whereas unit tests don't mandate when you write
tests. Without TDD, more often than not unit tests are written at the end of a
coding cycle to improve code coverage metrics. So, you can do unit testing
with or without TDD, but you can't do TDD without unit testing. Once you start
TDD, you will soon discover that it causes less pain than classic unit testing.

Value of TDD

We know that unit testing and testing in general help catch mistakes, but
why would we use TDD? There are several fundamental reasons. TDD
pushes the developer to write code for only what is minimally needed to
implement a feature, so it helps us shape our design to implement the
features required for actual or real use without any gold-plating in our
implementation—saving money and reducing complexity. We call this
YAGNI, or "you ain't gonna need it." It leads to much simpler code, as the
implementation is focused on what's required and not necessarily on what
you might be able to do.

In these days of faster mobile startups, YAGNI also encourages getting a
minimum viable product (MVP) out the door as quickly as possible. The
business owners choose the bare minimum of features needed to launch an
app in Google Play or the Amazon App Store. This minimum feature list is
then split into manageable chunks that feed your developer's TDD process.

Unit testing without practicing TDD can also get you a great regression test
suite that will help you avoid introducing any defects as you code. Because
we're writing unit tests before we write any code, the TDD regression test
suite is going to have more coverage and be much more comprehensive
than unit testing without TDD.

Also because of the ongoing refactoring, the code becomes more maintainable and much leaner, thereby leading to a longer life for your codebase. It is very easy to write horrible, untestable code in Android. Refactoring will encourage you to write small, focused, possibly single-line methods that are easily tested rather than monolithic Android views.

Finally, the process of coding in this continuous red/green/refactor cycle helps kill procrastination, as the focus is on small, discrete steps and the app gradually emerges from the bottom up as one feature after another is implemented.

Writing an App Using TDD

Before we get started we're going to need some basic requirements for our horoscope app.

- Display each star sign
- Display information about each star sign
- Display horoscope for star sign

There are lots of other things we could add, but we're practicing YAGNI so we're going to go with the minimum of features for our MVP horoscope app.

Feature 1

TDD means write the test first—which will fail—get the test to pass, and then refactor. Our first feature is to display each star sign. Create an Android app called Horoscope with an empty Activity using the Android wizard. Our first test uses Robolectric which we introduced in Chapter 3 to test that we have 12 signs displayed (see Listing 6-1).

Listing 6-1. Robolectric Test

```
@RunWith(RobolectricGradleTestRunner.class)
@Config(constants = BuildConfig.class, sdk = 21, manifest = "src/main/
AndroidManifest.xml")
public class ZodiacUnitTest {
    private Activity mainActivity;
    private ListView lstView;

    @Before
    public void setUp() {
        // Robolectric sets up the MainActivity class
        mainActivity= Robolectric.setupActivity(MainActivity.class);
        assertNotNull("Main Activity not setup",mainActivity);
```

```
    // add a listview to your layout file to get the test to compile
    lstView=(ListView)mainActivity.findViewById(R.id.list_of_signs);
}

@Test
public void shouldDisplaySigns() throws Exception {
    assertThat("should be a dozen star signs", 12, equalTo(lstView.
    getCount()));
}
}
```

The test code sets up a MainActivity and sees if we have 12 signs on our listView. Run the test and, of course, it fails (see Figure 6-1).

Figure 6-1. Test fails (red)

MainActivity.java (see Listing 6-2) has a ListView which uses the ListView item, list_of_signs, in our activity_main.xml layout file.

Listing 6-2. MainActivity.java

```
public class MainActivity extends AppCompatActivity {
    private Zodiac zodiac;
    private TextView mtxtSelectedItem;

    @Override
    protected void onCreate(Bundle savedInstanceState) {
        super.onCreate(savedInstanceState);
        setContentView(R.layout.activity_main);
        ListView listView = (ListView) findViewById(R.id.list_of_signs);
    }

}
```

The simplest way to get the code to compile is to add a zodiac_array in the strings.xml file (see Listing 6-3).

Listing 6-3. strings.xml

```
<resources>
    <string name="app_name">Horoscope</string>
    <string-array name="zodiac_array">
        <item>Aries</item>
        <item>Taurus</item>
        <item>Gemini</item>
        <item>Cancer</item>
        <item>Leo</item>
        <item>Virgo</item>
        <item>Libra</item>
        <item>Scorpio</item>
        <item>Sagittarius</item>
        <item>Capricorn</item>
        <item>Aquarius</item>
        <item>Pisces</item>
    </string-array>
</resources>
```

Now reference this array in the layout file (see Listing 6-4).

Listing 6-4. android_main.xml layout file

```
<ListView
        android:id="@+id/list_of_signs"
        android:entries="@array/zodiac_array"
        android:layout_width="fill_parent"
        android:layout_height="fill_parent" >
</ListView>
```

Run the test again and it passes (see Figure 6-2). Robolectric does take longer than vanilla unit tests to run but it's still seconds and not minutes. And we're getting Espresso test functionality without needing an emulator.

Figure 6-2. Test passes (green)

For this feature, we don't need to do any refactoring probably because the code is so limited. Instead we'll add more tests (see Listing 6-5).

Listing 6-5. Updated ZodiacUnitTests

```java
/**
 * If the Robolectric test will not run, edit the test configuration and add
\app to the
 * end of the Working Directory path (windows) or enter $MODULE_DIR$ (mac).
 */
@RunWith(RobolectricGradleTestRunner.class)
@Config(constants = BuildConfig.class, sdk = 21, manifest = "src/main/
AndroidManifest.xml")
public class ZodiacUnitTest {
    private ListView listView;
    private String[] zodiacSigns;

    @Before
    public void setUp() {
        MainActivity mainActivity = Robolectric.buildActivity(MainActivity.
        class).create().get();
        assertNotNull("Main Activity not setup", mainActivity);
        listView=(ListView) mainActivity.findViewById(R.id.list_of_signs);
        zodiacSigns = RuntimeEnvironment.application.getResources().
        getStringArray(R.array.zodiac_array);
    }

    @Test
    public void listLoaded() throws Exception {
        assertThat("should be a dozen star signs", zodiacSigns.length,
            equalTo(listView.getCount()));
    }
    @Test
    public void listContentCheck() {
        ListAdapter listViewAdapter = listView.getAdapter();
        assertEquals(zodiacSigns[0], listViewAdapter.getItem(0));
        assertEquals(zodiacSigns[1], listViewAdapter.getItem(1));
        assertEquals(zodiacSigns[2], listViewAdapter.getItem(2));
        assertEquals(zodiacSigns[3], listViewAdapter.getItem(3));
        assertEquals(zodiacSigns[4], listViewAdapter.getItem(4));
        assertEquals(zodiacSigns[5], listViewAdapter.getItem(5));
        assertEquals(zodiacSigns[6], listViewAdapter.getItem(6));
        assertEquals(zodiacSigns[7], listViewAdapter.getItem(7));
        assertEquals(zodiacSigns[8], listViewAdapter.getItem(8));
        assertEquals(zodiacSigns[9], listViewAdapter.getItem(9));
        assertEquals(zodiacSigns[10], listViewAdapter.getItem(10));
        assertEquals(zodiacSigns[11], listViewAdapter.getItem(11));
    }
}
```

Figure 6-3 shows the app after the first feature is completed.

Figure 6-3. List of star signs

Feature 2

In feature 2 we want to "Display information about each star sign." We need to create the `Zodiac` class to store all our information. So, assume that we have the following variables declared (see Listing 6-6).

Listing 6-6. Zodiac Variables

```
private String name;
private String description;
private String symbol;
private String month;
```

We could store the information in a SQLite database but that's not a requirement, so we'll take the easiest route and instead store the zodiac sign information in a class. Our new unit tests are now shown in Listing 6-7.

Listing 6-7. Unit Tests

```
@Test
    public void zodiacSymbolTest() throws Exception {
        TextView symbolTextView = (TextView) zodiacDetailActivity.
        findViewById(R.id.symbol);
        assertEquals(Zodiac.signs[ARIES_SIGN_INDEX].getSymbol(),
        symbolTextView.getText().toString());
    }

    @Test
    public void zodialMonthTest() throws Exception {
        TextView monthTextView = (TextView) zodiacDetailActivity.
        findViewById(R.id.month);
        assertEquals(Zodiac.signs[ARIES_SIGN_INDEX].getMonth(),
        monthTextView.getText().toString());
    }

    @Test
    public void zodiacNameTest() {
        TextView nameTextView = (TextView) zodiacDetailActivity.
        findViewById(R.id.name);
        assertEquals(Zodiac.signs[ARIES_SIGN_INDEX].getName(), nameTextView.
        getText().toString());
    }
```

As expected, seeing as we're in the red part of the red/green/refactor TDD cycle, the unit tests all fail (see Figure 6-4).

Figure 6-4. New unit tests fail

Complete the Zodiac class (see Listings 6-8 and 6-9) to store the horoscope information.

Listing 6-8. Updated Zodiac Class

```
public class Zodiac {
    private String name;
    private String description;
    private String symbol;
    private String month;
```

```java
public static final Zodiac[] signs = {
        new Zodiac("Aries","Courageous and Energetic.", "Ram", "April"),
        new Zodiac("Taurus","Known for being reliable, practical,
        ambitious and sensual.", "Bull", "May"),
        new Zodiac("Gemini","Gemini-born are clever and intellectual.",
        "Twins", "June"),
        new Zodiac("Cancer","Tenacious, loyal and sympathetic.", "Crab", "July"),
        new Zodiac("Leo","Warm, action-oriented and driven by the desire
        to be loved and admired.", "Lion", "August"),
        new Zodiac("Virgo","Methodical, meticulous, analytical and
        mentally astute.", "Virgin", "September"),
        new Zodiac("Libra","Librans are famous for maintaining balance
        and harmony.", "Scales","October"),
        new Zodiac("Scorpio","Strong willed and mysterious.",
        "Scorpion", "November"),
        new Zodiac("Sagittarius","Born adventurers.", "Archer", "December"),
        new Zodiac("Capricorn","The most determined sign in the
        Zodiac.", "Goat", "January"),
        new Zodiac("Aquarius","Humanitarians to the core", "Water
        Bearer", "February"),
        new Zodiac("Pisces","Proverbial dreamers of the Zodiac.",
        "Fish", "March"),
};

private Zodiac(String name, String description, String symbol, String month) {
    this.name = name;
    this.description = description;
    this.symbol = symbol;
    this.month = month;
}

public String getDescription() { return description;  }

public String getName() { return name; }

public String getSymbol() { return symbol; }

public String getMonth() { return month; }

public String toString() { return this.name; }

}
```

Listing 6-9. ZodiacDetailActivity class

```java
public class ZodiacDetailActivity extends Activity {

    public static final String EXTRA_SIGN = "ZodiacSign";

    @Override
    protected void onCreate(Bundle savedInstanceState) {
        super.onCreate(savedInstanceState);
        setContentView(R.layout.activity_zodiac_detail);

        int signNum = (Integer) getIntent().getExtras().get(EXTRA_SIGN);
        Zodiac zodiac = Zodiac.signs[signNum];

        TextView name = (TextView) findViewById(R.id.name);
        name.setText(zodiac.getName());

        TextView description = (TextView) findViewById(R.id.description);
        description.setText(zodiac.getDescription());

        TextView symbol = (TextView) findViewById(R.id.symbol);
        symbol.setText(zodiac.getSymbol());

        TextView month = (TextView) findViewById(R.id.month);
        month.setText(zodiac.getMonth());
    }
}
```

Run the tests and they now pass (see Figure 6-5).

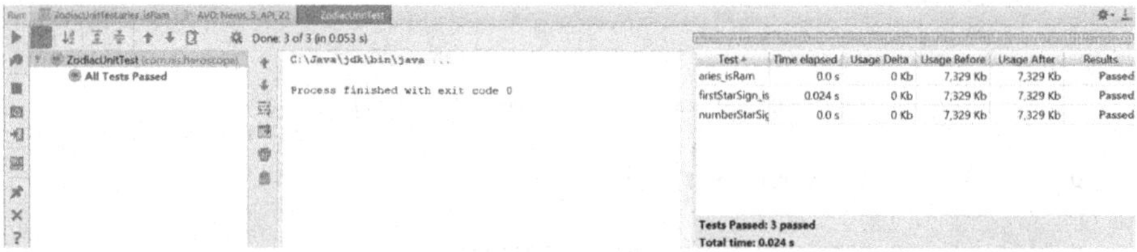

Figure 6-5. Zodiac unit tests pass

A lot has happened in this feature. The obvious refactoring step would be to put the information stored in Zodiac.java into a SQLite database. That doesn't add anything to our discussion so you can find the refactored code with the rest of source code at the Apress website.

The feature is now complete (see Figure 6-6).

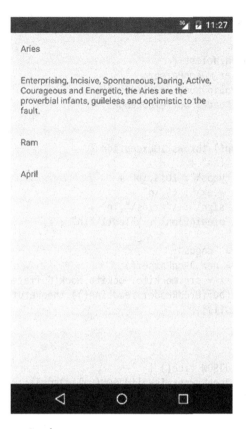

Figure 6-6. Information on star sign

Feature 3

Feature 3 says we should display the horoscope for star sign. So once again, let's start with the testing. The requirement is that it has got to be free and available in XML or JSON (Java Script Object Notation). We can create our own simple API or use one of the many free APIs from http://fabulously40.com or http://findyourfate.com.

We're going to use an API that calls the Onion's horoscope from http://a.knrz.co/horoscope-api.

We know from our Mockito examples in Chapter 4 that we're not going to test any network communication and testing our AyncTask methods is not something we want to do in our unit testing. But we should be testing our own methods that manipulate the returned horoscopes JSON (see Listing 6-10).

Listing 6-10. JSON Testing

```
@SmallTest
public class DailyZodiacTest {
    private JsonParser mJsonParser;
    private String validJson, invalidJson;
    private BufferedReader bufferedReader;

    @Before
    public void setUp() throws IOException {
        validJson = "{\n" +
                "  \"year\": 2015,\n" +
                "  \"week\": 45,\n" +
                "  \"sign\": \"aries\",\n" +
                "  \"prediction\": \"Test1\"\n" +
                "}";
        invalidJson = "bogus";
        mJsonParser = new JsonParser();
        bufferedReader = org.mockito.Mockito.mock(BufferedReader.class);
        Mockito.when(bufferedReader.readLine()).thenReturn(validJson).
        thenReturn(null);
    }

    @Test
    public void validJSON_true() {
        assertTrue(mJsonParser.isValidJSON(validJson));
    }

    @Test
    public void invalidJSON_false() {
        assertFalse(mJsonParser.isValidJSON(invalidJson));
    }

    @Test
    public void testCreateJsonObjectReturnsJsonObject() throws JSONException {
        JSONObject jsonObject = mJsonParser.createJsonObject(bufferedReader);
        String horoscope = jsonObject.getString("prediction");
        assertEquals("Test1", horoscope);
    }
}
```

The tests fail and we write the code to make them pass by creating the createJsonObject and isValidJson method in a new class called JsonParser (see Listing 6-11).

Listing 6-11. Valid JSON Code

```
protected JSONObject createJsonObject(BufferedReader reader) {
      try {
          StringBuilder sb = new StringBuilder();
          JSONObject jsonObject;
          String line;
          String json;

          while ((line = reader.readLine()) != null) {
              sb.append(line).append("\n");
          }

          json = sb.toString();
          jsonObject = new JSONObject(json);

          return jsonObject;
      } catch (Exception e) {
          Log.e(TAG, "Error converting result " + e.toString());
      }

      return null;
  }

  public boolean isValidJSON(String horoscope){
          try {
                  new JSONObject(horoscope);
                  return true;
          } catch (JSONException e) {
          e.printStackTrace();
                  return false;
          }
  }
```

Run the tests again and they pass. As the API call relies on is AsyncTask code, we cannot easily test it using unit testing. The recommended approach would be to test it via the emulator using Espresso.

This time, during the refactoring phase, there is a significant amount of other infrastructure code in our ZodiacDetailActivity class to get the horoscope to show up on the page.

The app now shows the horoscope on ZodiacDetailActivity (see Figure 6-7).

Figure 6-7. Horoscope app

Summary

In this chapter we created a simple three feature Horoscope app using TDD. In the first two features we used Robolectric in our tests and we used Mockito in the last feature. The unit testing code is limited to code that doesn't directly relate to the Android framework. At all times we avoided using any Espresso emulator testing to help keep the testing as rapid as possible.

Chapter 7

Dealing with Legacy Code

It's rare during your development career to have the luxury of being able to start with a clean slate every time you begin a new project. More often than not you're going to have to extend code written by someone else. Other times you're simply joining the team to help out with the increased workload. Inevitably, the temptation is just not to do any unit testing. After all, it's a massive task to create unit tests for the existing code, so why bother. But there are ways to approach this "no existing unit tests" scenario so that your code doesn't fall apart when the application gets to Quality Assurance (QA). "It's not my code" never was a very good excuse.

The process we take to introduce tests is as follows:

- Introduce continuous integration (CI) to build code
- Configure Android Studio for TDD (test-driven development)
- Add minimal unit tests based on existing tests and get them to run on a CI server
- Show team how to create unit tests
- Add testing code coverage metrics to CI, expect 5-10%
- Add Espresso tests
- Unit test any new features, while mocking existing objects

- ■ Isolate the existing code so nobody can access it directly;

- ■ Remove unused code

- ■ Refactor isolated code to get code coverage to ideally 60–70%

Whether you're the sole developer or part of a team it's always worth setting up a CI server. We looked at Jenkins earlier in the book, but you can use your own personal favorite as long as it integrates with Android and Gradle. Even if you do this step on its own, the team will see benefits.

Next add the JUnit, Mockito, and other dependencies to your project in Android Studio and make sure Studio is on the most recent stable version. Add some simple unit tests and show the team how to create unit tests so they get the general idea; show the team how unit tests work in the CI server. Code coverage at this step will be minimal.

Create Espresso tests for the basic functionality of the existing app—what are known as the primary use cases or happy path. You don't have the option of internally testing the app, but you can test it at the Activity level. Not doing this will lead to finger pointing if the app starts to fail and erode any confidence you've built in the new Agile development environment. Now that you've got this in place, create unit tests for any new code.

Don't edit the old code when adding new features. Isolate any old code so that no new code is added to your existing non-unit-tested/legacy code. Create interfaces to interact with the old code so it has a logical fence around it.

Finally once the development environment is stable you can begin to refactor the old code so that the code coverage is gradually increased over time. We'll look at how to accomplish this in the rest of this chapter using a tool called SonarQube.

SonarQube

Our goal is to refactor the code so it's easier to test and easier to maintain, but this can be problematic. For me Agile is about removing the blame and giving people the skills to implement quality features faster. Telling someone that their code smells isn't going to be an easy sell no matter how you package it so it's best to stay objective rather than subjective. Thankfully there are a number of tools and metrics —other than code coverage—that provide this objectivity. SonarQube can be particularly useful to identify real issues with the code.

Install SonarQube as follows:

1. Download and install SonarQube Server; use the
   most up to date LTS (long-term support) version,
   from www.sonarqube.org/downloads/.

2. Download and install the Sonar Runner.

3. Start the Sonar Server; run C:\sonarqube\bin\
   windows-x86-xx\StartSonar.bat on Windows or
   /etc/sonarqube/bin/[OS]/sonar.sh console on Unix.

4. Go to http://localhost:9000 in your browser to see
   if the Sonar Dashboard is running (see Figure 7-1).

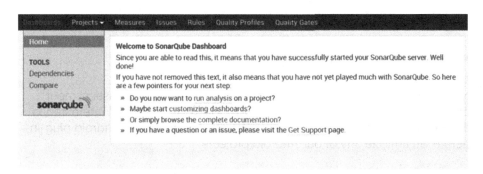

Figure 7-1. SonarQube Dashboard

We need to check that the server is analyzing projects and the Java plug-in
is installed, so download the Sonar examples.

1. Download the Sonar examples from https://github.
   com/SonarSource/sonar-examples/archive/master.
   zip and unzip

2. To get the project information into the Sonar
   Dashboard we need to use the runner. Navigate to
   the java example folder and start the runner, cd
   C:\sonar-examples\projects\languages\java\sonar-
   runner\java-sonar-runner-simple and then run
   C:\sonar-runner\bin\sonar-runner.bat or on Unix
   cd /etc/sonar-examples/projects/languages/java/
   sonar-runner/java-sonar-runner-simple and run
   the /etc/sonar-runner/bin/sonar-runner command.

3. Navigate to the Sonar Dashboard, click the Java project and you should see the image in Figure 7-2.

Figure 7-2. Sonar analytics for our Java project

Note that we're getting a "C" grade for our Software Quality Assessment based on Lifecycle Expectations (SQLAE). However, we're not interested in this project as it is Java, not Android. We need to install the Android plug-in before we analyze any of our Android projects.

1. Log in as Administrator using admin/admin

2. Click Settings ➤ Update Center ➤ Available Plugins (see Figure 7-3).

Figure 7-3. Sonar Update Center

3. Click the Android Lint plug-in to install the plug-in and restart SonarQube.

The Android plug-in will import any lint errors into SonarQube as well as allow you to navigate any Java errors. To see the sample Android project, do the following:

1. `cd C:\sonar-examples\projects\languages\android\android-sonarqube-runner` or on Unix `/etc/sonar-examples/projects/languages/android/android-sonarqube-runner`

2. Create the bin/classes folder as it fails to load without creating the directory

3. Run `C:\sonar-runner\bin\sonar-runner.bat` or on unix `/etc/sonar-runner/bin/sonar-runner`

Figure 7-4 shows the top-level analysis on this basic project.

Figure 7-4. *Android app analysis*

Install the Tab Metrics plug-in as above and restart SonarQube. Even though it's on a very small project, when you now click the Issues link (see Figure 7-5), you should get a flavor of the issues that SonarQube identifies.

Figure 7-5. Android app issues list

The Android plug-in works great for Android apps written in Eclipse which will probably be the majority of legacy apps you're trying to fix. Now that we have that working, we should install the Gradle plug-in so we can analyze Android Studio projects.

1. Add the plug-in and `sonarProperties` to your `build.gradle` (app) file, see Listing 7-1. This won't replace the existing file but will be in addition to what's already in the file.

2. Click Sync Now to update the `build.gradle` file.

3. Run your Analyzer command from the project root directory with the command `gradlew sonarRunner`.

4. Open the dashboard at `http://localhost:9000`, to browse your project's quality.

Listing 7-1. build.gradle Updates

```
apply plugin: 'sonar-runner'

sonarRunner{
    sonarProperties{
        property "sonar.host.url", "http://localhost:9000"
        property "sonar.jdbc.url", "jdbc:mysql://localhost:3306/sonar?use
        Unicode=true&characterEncoding=utf8&rewriteBatchedStatements=true&use
        Configs=maxPerformance"
        property "sonar.jdbc.driverClassName","com.mysql.jdbc.Driver"
        property "sonar.jdbc.username","root"
        property "sonar.jdbc.password","root"
```

```
    property "sonar.projectKey", "RIIS:CropCompare"
    property "sonar.projectVersion", "2.0"
    property "sonar.projectName","CropCompare"
    property "sonar.java.coveragePlugin", "jacoco"
    property "sonar.sources","src\\main"
    property "sonar.tests", "src\\test"
    property "sonar.jacoco.reportPath", "build\\jacoco\\jacocoTest.exec"
    property "sonar.java.binaries", "build"
    property "sonar.dynamicAnalysis", "resuseReports"
  }
}
```

Figure 7-6 shows the CropCompare app has almost 200 issues – 47 Critical and 87 Major - that need to be fixed.

Figure 7-6. *CropCompare app issues list*

Comparing Projects

When you have got the code coverage up to something that you consider respectable, you might to use the Sonar compare projects functionality to see how each of the projects compares (see Figure 7-7). We can quickly identify what projects have poor code coverage and also the high complexity. This will quickly identify other projects that need to undergo the same process.

| sonarqube | Dashboards ▾ | Issues | Measures | Rules | Quality Profiles | Quality Gates | More ▾ |

Compare

| Add metric ▾ | | Add project ▾ |

	CropCompare 2.0 Nov 04 2015	ContextIO Android 1.0 Oct 05 2015
Lines of code	913	3,127
Complexity	148	195
Comments (%)	6.8%	18.7%
Duplicated lines (%)	14.0%	21.5%
Issues	199	288
Coverage		9.7%

Figure 7-7. Comparing projects

Refactor Code

Once you've fixed the SonarQube issues, you should have slimmed down the largest classes and removed the critical code smell issues. Remember to test the code using your Espresso test suite after any major surgery to make sure you haven't broken the build.

Refactoring may also involve creating a new, cleaner architecture for your project. MVP (model-view-presenter) and MVVM (model-view-viewmodel) are both becoming popular Android architectures. Data Binding is another great way to clean up your code—although at time of writing it's still in beta—as it removes the data references from the user interface or UI and is also a good first step in implementing an MVVM architecture.

Lessons Learned

Before we finish this chapter it would be a mistake to not talk about a few lessons learned during the transition from poorly written legacy Android code to something more maintainable.

Keep the conversations objective. Telling someone that his code is bad is a very subjective conversation. But telling the team that the goal is to have code coverage and complexity metrics at the same level as the different projects on the company's Git server is a much easier sell.

Don't ship any tests or test information with your app. It's unlikely in the current unit testing environment that you'd be able to include unit tests in your APK (Android application package) even if you tried, but we've seen many examples of test data being stored in resources and assets folders in the past, so always unzip your production APK to ensure it doesn't have anything extra in the payload.

Take baby steps when you inherit an existing project. Don't be driven by metrics. Try not to get too worried about code coverage; after all, you're being judged on how you write good clean code that delivers value, not if your code coverage or any other metric is more than some specific value.

It's important to also keep an eye on performance metrics. Just like the Espresso test harness, some simple app timing metrics will keep you on track. There is nothing worse than creating quality-tested code to find it's two or three times slower than the original legacy code. There is no reason it should be, but mistakes happen so add a performance metric so you can become aware of it (and it can be eradicated) before it becomes an issue.

Add some configuration time to your estimates. If done correctly, manual QA hours should decrease considerably, but this means that the development and devops time will eat up some of that gain. Don't assume the developers are going to go full on TDD without a configuration learning curve.

Summary

In this chapter we've looked at some strategies for adding unit testing to an existing code base. Using Sonar and refactoring in Android Studio, over time you can gradually decouple existing apps, increase their code coverage, and decrease their complexity.

Finally, it's worth stating that you don't need anyone's permission to unit test, even if the rest of the team does not want to partake. Right now you can start unit testing using Android Studio as there are no longer any impediments to beginning unit testing as the rest of the Java world has been doing for about a decade. With or without TDD, unit testing needs to become part of your development process.

Index

Get the eBook for only $5!

Why limit yourself?

Now you can take the weightless companion with you wherever you go and access your content on your PC, phone, tablet, or reader.

Since you've purchased this print book, we're happy to offer you the eBook in all 3 formats for just $5.

Convenient and fully searchable, the PDF version enables you to easily find and copy code—or perform examples by quickly toggling between instructions and applications. The MOBI format is ideal for your Kindle, while the ePUB can be utilized on a variety of mobile devices.

To learn more, go to www.apress.com/companion or contact support@apress.com.

Printed in the United States
By Bookmasters